Liberator Pilot: The Cottontails' Battle for Oil

Liberator Pilot: The Cottontails' Battle for Oil

by
Vincent F. Fagan

California Aero Press
Carlsbad, California

Cover art courtesy of:

International B-24 Liberator Club
P.O. Box 15-2424
San Diego, CA 92195

Typesetting by Shelley Fagan, Tempe, Arizona

CALIFORNIA AERO PRESS
P.O. Box 1365
Carlsbad, CA 92018

Library of Congress Catalog Card Number 91-70428
ISBN 0-914379-02-X

Printed in the United States of America

This book is for

James L. Estes — good night, sweet prince

and

Jack C. Evans — may his tribe increase.

"AS FLAK GOES BY"

(Mournfully - to the tune of "As Time Goes By")

You must remember this
The Flak can't always miss
Somebody's gotta die.
The odds are always too damned high
As Flak goes by.

And when the fighters come
You hope you're not the one
To tumble from the sky.
The odds are always too damned high.
As Flak goes by.

110s and 210s knocking at the gate
-- sky full of fighters
Gotta kill that rate,
Salvo - don't delay
The target's passing by.

It's still the same old story
The Eighth gets all the glory
While we're the ones who die.
The odds are always too damned high.
As Flak goes by.

Anonymous

The End

Innsbruck, Austria, December 25, 1944 (Vincent Fagan collection)

Christmas Day 1944, clear, bright and beautiful.

We arched up from the southeast and flattened out at twenty-seven thousand feet over the Alps and headed out toward the main railroad marshalling yard at Innsbruck, Austria. Innsbruck is on the north side of the Alps at the head of Brenner Pass and is the focal point for all rail operations south into Italy.

All supplies for the German Army in Italy had to come through the Brenner Pass from Germany -- the trains were assembled in Innsbruck before being run through the pass into Italy.

The Fifteenth Air Force had tried all kinds of things to

i

stop this traffic. We bombed various bridges inside the Brenner Pass and the freight yards in Innsbruck. All without success.

Part of the problem was that when you bombed a bridge or a freight yard you could blow it up but it could be reassembled and put back in operation very rapidly.

It was frustrating, but we had to try again or at least keep things screwed up for a while.

My crew has two replacements today. Driggs, our bombardier, had been hurt and was replaced by Lt. Moe Hallins, a navigator, on his second mission. Bob Felker, my co-pilot, had been given his own crew and has been replaced by Lt. Ned March. Ned had been out of action for some time, having been hit in the cheek bone by a fifty caliber cartridge ejected by a tail gunner in front of him while he was flying number four position. The heavy cartridge came through the windshield and hit him with tremendous force.

This was my 41st mission. Rod East, the engineer, and "Pappy" Van Lowell, the ball turret gunner and radio operator, are on their last, their 50th mission. They picked up nine missions on me when I was in the hospital.

Spaak was in the tail turret, Olean in the nose and Hart and Cool on the waist guns.

We hit the I.P. and began a straight in bomb run to the target. We are flying number two position in what was called the X-ray One box. Our group and our seven ship box are leading the 15th Air Force today.

I had been to Innsbruck twice before and I felt pretty

good about the mission. The flak wasn't all that heavy and we should be in and out of it in a hurry. We were flying "Maiden America".

We started down the bomb run with flak breaking all around us; I got a call from the waist that our #1 engine was hit and pouring gasoline out in a steady stream.

The engine seemed to be putting out power but I didn't like the idea of 100 octane fuel streaming a few inches past a white hot turbo super charger wheel on the rear, underside of the engine nacelle. This is the sort of thing that could turn you into a high altitude roman candle.

A few more seconds and bombs went away -- we rallied hard right, and then all hell broke loose. Several violent explosions racked the ship; a large piece of flak slammed into my chest, stopped by my flak jacket, as Ned and I were showered with powdered plexiglass from various pieces of flak which crashed through the windshield.

The plane staggered, and barely under control, started a slow downward turn to the left; incredibly, we spiraled through the seven ship box without hitting anyone as the other six planes continued rallying right.

One clever type called me. "Merry Christmas, Vince". I didn't hear him -- the radios were shot out. The instrument panel was also shot to pieces. The only operative instruments left were the air speed indicator, altimeter, climb and dive indicator and cylinder head temperature. All the gyros were gone, compasses out and other engine instruments out.

I jumped on the right rudder with both feet and wound in full rudder trim. The turn to the left began to slow. I rolled full right aileron into it and the left wing came up in what would normally be a forty-five degree bank.

In this attitude, the plane stopped turning and maintained a straight course, almost due west, I estimated -- the sun being about ninety degrees to our left and it being 12:00 noon. We had done a one hundred eighty degree turn since we were hit; and, unfortunately, we were losing altitude at the rate of five thousand feet per minute. We were about ten miles north of Innsbruck at this time, and I could see a tremendous, gratifying, column of smoke coming up from the center of the city.

A wave of despondency swept over me. I couldn't believe this was happening to us. We were going down as sure as hell.

We weren't going to make it back no matter what we did and there were no clever, tricky maneuvers we could pull off that would save our butts.

We were going down and quick. Losing 5,000 feet per minute, we had about five minutes till we'd be walking.

The possibility of fire or explosion from the various gas leaks was a large, looming negative factor.

Ned March, the co-pilot, had apparently been hit in the arm -- his sleeve was torn, but he never said anything. He was, however, unable to help.

Rod East, the engineer, was in the upper deck turret and had been hit in the neck and in the leg. He climbed down on the flight deck to seek help.

Instead, he found more trouble. He found that the fuel sight gauges had been shot out and were spurting gasoline all over the flight deck. He climbed out onto the bomb bay catwalk, with the bomb bay doors open, so he could be at the petcocks to shut off the sight gauges.

A foot of gas line had been shot out in the bomb bay, spraying gasoline all over the place. Rod went back to the flight deck for his tool box, cut off a length of spare hose, went back and taped in a replacement length of hose.

When you consider that Rod did all this while he was wounded, above twenty thousand feet without oxygen, standing on a six inch catwalk with no parachute, with the temperature below minus thirty degrees fahrenheit, and all the time being sprayed with gasoline, you have to conclude that this was a remarkable accomplishment; the type of determined, resourceful action that can keep a plane in the air when badly damaged.

A call from the waist advised me that there was a six-inch hole in the left wing behind the number two engine, and gas was streaming out of the hole. Apparently, we had caught a direct hit from an 88mm shell and the contact fuse had been a dud. Gas also was still streaming out of the number one engine.

The cylinder head temperature gauges indicated that both number one and number two engines were out, so I tried to feather the propeller on both of them. No dice. They wouldn't feather. We'd have to let them continue to windmill, causing substantial drag. Like driving with your emergency brake on.

I could see ten or fifteen flak holes in the cowling of the number two engine, and the cowling and prop were covered with oil. If the prop continued to windmill till the oil supply was exhausted, the engine would eventually build up enough heat to tear itself to pieces. The most important thing at this stage of the game was to get as far away from Innsbruck as possible.

According to intelligence, the civilians at Innsbruck and Munich were hanging captured air crewmen, if they got their hands on them. If we could get fifteen or twenty miles out into the country we'd probably be all right, especially if we could get captured by soldiers, who would rarely mistreat you.

The gas leakage worried me because of the possibility of getting whacked with some tracer bullets from a German fighter which were plentiful hereabout. I called the gunners and told them to get out of their turrets and put on their chutes; to watch out very carefully for fighters. We couldn't risk even one enemy pass, we'd have to drop the gear and jump if a plane showed up.

We were at 19,000 feet and still losing 5,000 feet per minute -- in less than four minutes we'd be on the ground; there was no way out -- we were going down.

Down,
Down,
Goddamit, down.

PROLOGUE

Morning Star, a 450th Bomb Group Liberator over Italy following its 100th Mission. The Lib crashed on its third landing attempt, killing four crewmen. November 1944. (Courtesy San Diego Aerospace Museum)

First the reminiscences, then the discussion and finally the argument.

The question was: which was the most important ingredient for survival in combat -- luck or skill.

The argument came about when I bumped into an old friend from cadet days, Robert Thomason, on an airline flight from the east coast to St. Louis in the late fifties.

We discussed mutual friends for a while, then the fact that he had washed out of Primary Flight Training at Muskogee and spent the rest of the war as a company clerk at Sheppard Field in Wichita Falls, Texas.

I told him that I had graduated from twin engine advanced at Altus, Oklahoma, and wound up as a B-24 first pilot in the 15th Air Force in Manduria, Italy.

"What was it like, flying combat?" he asked.

"Grimsville."

"What was the situation on casualties? What percent of the crews got shot down?" were the next questions.

"I really don't know," I replied, "I don't have any figures even for our own bomb group, except that I went overseas with thirty-three crews, three hundred thirty men; and out of this group, twenty-two crews went down. In the case of my own crew, I had five men killed."

"Most of the crews seemed to go down in the first ten missions or the last ten missions -- the first ten primarily because of inexperience, the last ten because it seemed that the law of averages began to catch up with you." I continued.

"You needed a lot of luck at the start to keep you alive until you knew what was going on, from then on you could pretty well control the situation through skill, knowledge, experience or whatever you chose to call it. I'll lump all these under the term 'experience'.

"No matter how much training you got in the states, you were never fully prepared for combat -- they simply didn't have time to train you for the different circumstances you'd find flying in England, the Aleutians, the Himalayas, the South Pacific or wherever you wound up," I said.

"But wasn't it strictly luck whether a crew went down or

not?" Robert asked.

"No," I replied, "after about 15 or 20 missions, you are thoroughly familiar with the area you are flying in -- Southern Europe and the Balkans in my case -- and this is a tremendous advantage over a new crew who is not familiar with the area. I can still draw you a pretty good map of the Balkans with all the headings to and from various targets and our home base.

"Also after 8 or 10 missions I got my pick of the planes in the squadron. Out of 15 or 20 planes, I consistently got to fly what I considered the best airplane. This was a sizeable advantage over a crew just starting out, who consistently got the worst airplanes to fly or at least the leftovers.

"As you flew more missions your formation flying improved, which resulted in a substantial gas saving, greater safety, less effort on your part and less wear and tear on the engines.

"Experience brought better and safer landings and takeoffs and, in addition, the rest of the crew became more skilful and dependable in their jobs," I added. "Nobody lasts very long in combat unless he gets very cold-bloodedly efficient at what he's doing."

Robert dismissed these arguments as meaningless and no matter what I told him he remained convinced that survival in combat was 100% pure, blind luck.

I never saw Robert again but he was so insistent that his position was correct, and I felt he was so off base that the conversation has stayed with me ever since, finally resulting in this book. I resented his opinion which was based on his experience flying a desk in combat in Texas.

As a result of this discussion, I conducted a one man survey with anyone I met who had ever been in combat in any branch of service. The question being: which would they rather have in combat, luck or experience?

No one picked luck -- out of hundreds I questioned. Everyone wanted all the luck they could get their hands on, but the opportunities to get your head blown off seemed to be so numerous that luck could not carry you, except for a very short time.

Of the guys I talked to, most felt that the way to survive in combat was to avoid making mistakes. Unfortunately, in the beginning you didn't know whether what you were doing was a mistake or not. The intelligent thing to do to shorten the learning period was to ask questions, though many newcomers were too proud to do this for various reasons.

It made me angry that this dumb son-of-a-bitch, Robert, could be so certain about something he knew so little about. Yet upon reflection it occurred to me that, in the beginning, I thought it was all luck, too.

When I arrived in Naples in July, 1944, we met crews who had finished their tour and were going home. Some of them I knew personally, and trusted what they told us to be true; the consensus was that combat was ten times rougher than they had expected and the losses much greater.

Since I had very little flying experience, less than 500 hours total and no combat experience, the only thing for me to hang my hat on for survival, was luck. The more I heard about difficulties ahead, the more I assumed a rabbit's foot complex. Dumb blind luck was my only ally.

I call this the Clay Pigeon Theory.

It seems to you that the Air Force whips up twenty-eight airplanes from each group and ships them off on a mission; they fly over the targets and the enemy shoots at them with planes and flak. On the average a couple of planes get knocked down each trip. From this standpoint, it *is* all luck -- whoever takes a direct hit and blows up, whoever had a wing shot off or catches on fire, has had it, no matter how experienced or skilled.

This view, while correct as far as it goes, applies mainly to the bomb run and ignores all the dangers normally associated with flying and compounded in combat -- crashing on takeoffs or landings, getting lost, running out of gas, midair collisions, formation flying, bad weather and finally, battle damage that permits you to get out of the target area but unable to get all the way back.

This last, in my opinion, would be the largest category of losses.

These difficulties are things that you can improve your ability to handle and get better at with experience. After my crew had been flying missions for a while, we found many ways to create a better set of odds for ourselves so that by the end of my tour I thought that combat survival was about eighty-five or ninety percent experience and about ten or fifteen percent luck.

I was scared pea green when I started, as was everyone else; but by the time I was finishing my tour, I was extremely confident and so was my crew; I had the utmost confidence in them and our ability to handle almost any emergency. Combat is something in which you start out awfully scared and lonely and wind up very cold and calculating. Anyone who gets in the way of survival, friend or foe, cut 'em off at the knees.

I thought we could handle anything except a fire or a direct hit and a resulting explosion, and I thought the chance of these happening were fairly remote.

Robert is entitled to his opinion; but it is my belief that almost any individual, no matter how inexperienced and apprehensive he may be, could learn to control the initial fear and panic -- which he is bound to have on his first few missions -- and as soon as he does this, he could then start looking around for ways to improve the odds in his favor.

This is the beginning of wisdom and survival.

It is not my intention to attempt to prove either the luck or skill theory but simply to record some of my impressions of heavy bombardment flying in Italy in World War II.

Some stories reflect almost pure luck, others almost all skill.

In the following, several individual's names have been changed for various obvious or obscure reasons, and so has the locale of several stories.

1.

Two 450th Bomb Group B-24s coast out after a raid on
Theole-sur-mar, France, July 12, 1944.

Hannibal watered his elephants in Manduria in 212
B.C. By 1944, the Americans were there with their Big
Iron Bird, the B-24 Liberator, four engine bomber.

The 450th bomb Group was stationed at an old Italian
fighter base about four or five miles east of town, in the
heel of the Italian boot, about midway between Taranto
and Brindisi. The code name of the field was "Frantic".

It was a miserable set-up. Dusty, scraggly, carved out
of a huge olive grove and surrounded by a decrepit rock
wall; the runway was oiled dirt with large chuck holes

and the few buildings had been unpainted for years --
straight out of Tobacco Road.

There were no hangars for servicing airplanes -- all
maintenance was done in the open air -- summer and
winter. There were some old Italian barracks, jerry-built
and appearing to be in imminent danger of collapse.
The twenty eight hundred Americans who lived here,
lived for the most part in G.I. tents; a few entrepreneurs
built stone houses. The balance who couldn't get a tent
or a house inhabited the barracks.

There was an open air movie theater, an Officer's Club
and several mess halls and administration buildings
inherited from the Italians.

If this was what a victorious army looked like in action
-- what a shattering thought to reflect on what a losing
German Army must look like.

Most of us thought the dust was pretty bad in summer
until we saw the mud in winter. Winter was cold -- it
snowed in December -- and was made even more
difficult because there was only about six inches of red
clay on top of a solid slab of limestone; and as a
consequence, huge pools of standing rain water formed,
some five hundred to one thousand feet in diameter,
during the winter months, hindering transit and causing
the base to be re-named "Lake Frantic".

My crew and eleven other newly arrived replacement
crews from the States were assigned here and duly
delivered by truck from the repple depot at Gioia di
Colle, at the end of July, 1944.

The pilots were immediately ordered to report to the

briefing room to hear a few words from the Group Commanding Officer, Colonel "Fearless Red" McGuirk, also known as the "The Meanest Man in Italy".

It was customary for the C.O. to greet newly arrived pilots at any base with a few words of welcome, usually something to the effect that "we're happy to have you with us and you'll like it here."

No so with Fearless Red, West Point '39. He stood up on the stage in front of the twenty-four pilots and co-pilots flanked by the Group Intelligence Officer and Group Flight Surgeon, staring at us intently for a moment and then he spoke: "Gentlemen, you are fresh meat," said McGuirk. "I'm sorry to put it to you that way, but that is the way it is.

"This bomb squadron is exhausted -- we have flown thirteen missions in the last fifteen days; 723rd Squadron is down to five crews when they should have twenty.

"Normally we would send you out as co-pilots with experienced crews but there is not time for that now. Tomorrow we will fly you on an orientation flight around the field and the following day, you'll fly your first mission.

"The name of the game here is formation flying," he continued, "if you fly good formation, everything more or less takes care of itself. One B-24 cannot hold off one Me-109, but 28 B-24s in good formation can hold off 10,000 Me-109s.

"We fly a seven-ship combat box, a three-plane Vee in front, another three-plane Vee stepped down about ten feet below and to the rear, a tail-end-charlie bring up the ass end. This gives us about six times the fire power of an attacking fighter.

"Each squadron puts up seven planes for each mission and we then fly a group formation of four seven ship boxes.

"As I said, the key to success in combat is good, tight formation, for fighter protection and for bombing patterns because we toggle our bombs on the leader who normally bombs with radar. Many times enemy fighters will come by and look over the various formations and pick out the worst ones to clobber -- so it pays to keep in close.

"Which brings up the question of how much high altitude formation flying you have had in training. Those of you who have had twenty hours or more above twenty thousand feet, raise your hands."

No response.

"Ten hours above twenty thousand feet?"

No response again.

"Any time at all above sixteen thousand feet?"

Nothing.

I had had about three hours, but I didn't feel this was the time to strike up an acquaintance with Fearless Red.

"What the goddam hell are they doing back there in the States -- teaching you all to be airline pilots? By God, you'll learn how to fly high altitude formation here, and goddam quick or else."

Fearless Red's face kept getting redder and his voice louder as he continued, "Another reason for formation flying is that, unfortunately, we have no radio letdown or takeoff facilities here. Only a voice tower, so that when you return from a mission and the field is socked in, the lead ship lets down with radar over the Adriatic, and then we hedge-hop back to the field under the soup and the radar ship locates the field.

"We come down the runway about 100 feet off the ground; the number three ship pulls up in a forty-five degree bank, followed by the number one and number two man, etc. As soon as your gear and flaps are down, you start letting down; and when you have completed a three hundred sixty degree turn, find yourself on the runway."

This sounded hair-raising to me and it was, when I tried it; but it worked. I must have later made a dozen landings like this in ceilings as low as two hundred feet. Even if we had letdown facilities, runway localizers and the like, we couldn't have used them anyway because there wasn't time to go through the procedures involved. Everyone was too low on gas at the end of a mission to go through a standard instrument letdown procedure. We never had an accident while I was with the group using this system, but McGuirk was right. You'd better stay in good, tight formation from the Adriatic back to the field; and once you peeled off and started your turn, keep it as tight as you could so no one could get inside your turn and cut you out of the pattern. No one wanted to go around with almost no gas.

When you had to make an instrument takeoff, you simply took off and climbed till you got on top and then flew the race track pattern, a long oval pattern, till you got in formation. There was some danger from the other twenty-seven planes involved in this, but there were never any collisions. It didn't matter how low the ceiling or how much rain, we took off for a mission using this system regardless of the weather.

Fearless Red continued, "Here are a few things that may help you. Back in the states they taught you what to do in the way of emergency procedure in case an engine catches on fire. Personally, I've never seen anybody put out a fire on a B-24; and if one I'm flying catches fire, I'm going to jump immediately.

"If you want to go through all that emergency procedure crap before you jump, it's alright with me. You only have about four or five seconds to get out though."

Bob Felker, my co-pilot, sitting next to me, leaned over and muttered, "A B-24 is just a big bonfire going somewhere to happen."

Fearless Red continued, "If you lose an engine or two and can't keep up, just do the best you can. No one from the group will stay with you to help. That just makes two stragglers. If you're lucky, you may pick up some fighter escort. If not, just stay with it as long as you can.

"If you are jumped by a German fighter, don't try to be a hero -- you might take one pass from him just to make sure that he's got some ammunition, then drop your gear to indicate surrender and bail out.

"Incidentally, we can land on the Isle of Vis off the coast of Yugo just opposite Split. It's held by the Partisans and has a three thousand foot runway -- long enough to land on, but too short to take off. You'll be brought back by boat or light plane."

I later found out that there were deep gullies at each end of this runway that were obscured by grape vines which made it very dangerous to overshoot the runway or extend your landing roll -- that is was far better to ground loop if necessary than go off the runway. This intelligence came from a crew I met in the hospital who had overrun the end of the runway.

"We have four picket boats in the Adriatic. If you have to ditch, try and get as close to one of them as possible and they'll try to pick you up," McGuirk said.

"If you are knocked out of formation and unsure of your position, call 'Big Fence.' It's a radio D.F. outfit that will give you a no wind magnetic heading back here to Frantic. Be careful not to call them north of Venice -- the Germans will give you a heading to lead you over Venice and then blow the hell out of you.

"Most crews go down in Yugoslavia coming back from the target. If you are picked up by the Chetnicks or Partisans, you will probably get out alive. If you are picked up by the Ustachi or Germans, you will probably be killed on the spot. Unfortunately, no one is taking any prisoners in Yugo. Personally, I'd carry my .45 and not let myself be captured by the Ustachi or Germans.

"You will be furnished with escape kits, maps, morphine and forty-eight American dollars before each mission. As soon as we can, we will take pictures of each of you in civilian clothes to use on phoney passports if you go down in France.

"You may not bomb anywhere in Northern Italy, France or Yugoslavia unless it is an assigned mission by the Bomb Group. However, you may bomb indiscriminately in Germany, Austria, Czechoslovakia, Hungary, Bulgaria and Rumania."

And he did mean indiscriminately. By the end of the War, fighter planes were strafing people on bicycles in Germany; anything that moved was fair game.

"One final word. About combat fatigue. There are only two diseases you can get which can cause combat fatigue. They are the screaming meemies, and the Chinese rot, and in order to be grounded in this outfit, you must have them both simultaneously. However, medical science says that it is impossible to have these two diseases simultaneously. Isn't that right, Captain?" he said turning to the Group Flight Surgeon.

The flight surgeon stammered, got red in the face, watching his Hippocratic oath being strangled in front of him, and agreed that this was so.

"So you are going to fly your missions by God, come hell or high water and you can forget about combat fatigue; you can forget about getting grounded for any reason," he thundered.

"That's all."

Fearless Red turned and walked out of the room.

While this guy sounded and looked like a very rough customer, I had to admit that his advice seemed sensible -- at least he wasn't counseling any heroic measures to save the airplane if you were on fire or were jumped by fighters.

8

I couldn't believe that a West Point graduate could be so rude, crude and uncultured as McGuirk. He looked and sounded a lot like Wallace Berry, except that alongside McGuirk, Berry seemed a little effeminate.

Also, his stated policy on combat fatigue wasn't true -- it was inconsistent as hell, various guys got out of flying combat in various ways.

Fearless Red was far too fearless for my taste. I had the misfortune later to fly with him on his last mission. He was leading the box in which I was flying, and we were to bomb some oil installations at Moosbierbaum on the north edge of the Vienna flak area.

Everyone was happy about the proposed mission. We would get a double mission credit for going to Vienna. We would come up from the south, fly around the western edge of the flak area, then come in from the north; duck into the flak about one minute, bomb Moosbierbaum and duck out again. Unfortunately, that isn't the way Fearless Red did it.

After dropping our bombs on the target, instead of rallying hard left as he was supposed to do, Fearless Red continued straight ahead for about five minutes and then started a slow, leisurely turn which took us over much of the hated and dangerous Vienna flak area.

Everyone, including the gunners, was on the radio screaming at him and demanding to know what the hell was going on. But no word came forth from our fearless leader. We finally slowly exited the flak area and proceeded back to Frantic.

After we landed, I went over to Bob Bryan, who was

9

flying co-pilot for McGuirk and asked him what had gone wrong. Bob said that since it was his last mission, McGuirk wanted to get some good flak pictures; so while Bob flew the slow turn, McGuirk took pictures. By the time the story circulated the bomb group, McGuirk had gone back to the States. If he had tried it again, he would have done it solo.

2.

The author's crew at the time of training, Boise, Idaho. Author is second from left, standing. (Vincent Fagan collection)

After Fearless Red's cheery welcome, I drifted over to the bar of the Officer's Club -- the home of the twenty-five cent cocktail -- cherry brandy, mixed with canned orange-grapefruit juice.

Next to me at the bar was a pilot with forty-five missions -- a genuine hot rock. I started talking to him and in the course of the conversation, I asked him how many planes the group put up each day.

"Twenty-eight each mission."

"Jesus Christ, how many planes does the group have?" I

11

asked.

"About sixty."

This was incredible.

The fondest dream of the training group at Boise was to put up an eighteen ship formation -- the most they ever got up at one time while I was there was eight. The maintenance was that bad. They could only get about one out of five airplanes in the air at one time.

I later learned the reason the 450th could do it; the ground crews worked 24 hours a day. I never went out to the flight line at any hour of the day or night that the mechanics were not out there working. These mechanics were the most dedicated people I ever saw. I am not overstating it when I say that they'd break down and cry when their plane went down. It always seemed they thought there was something else they could have done to make the plane more airworthy.

I asked my friendly hot rock about adjusting weight and balance.

"What do you mean?" he asked.

"You know, adjusting the weight so that the center of gravity is in the right place."

"You might as well forget that load adjusting crap. If you are taxiing out and the plane falls down on its tail, stand on the brakes, gun the engines and the nose will come down -- everything will be okay -- put three or four gunners up in the nose to level things out.

"As far as the total weight is concerned, you may as well know that these 24's are overloaded about eight or ten thousand pounds. Consolidated Aircraft says maximum takeoff weight is sixty-three thousand pounds. These planes weigh about seventy-three to seventy-five thousand pounds.

"If you don't like it, what do you want to leave behind? Machine gun ammunition? The flak suits? Take less gasoline? Or what? You're going to have to take the bombs or there's no point in going."

I asked him if you had to ask the group or squadron leader if you wanted to drop out of formation.

"Look", he replied, "Something you'd better get through your head is that the squadron leader is just another guy up front trying to save his ass. You do whatever you think is best for yourself and the hell with him."

The beginning of wisdom.

I had been in the Army for eighteen months, and all that time I had been training with someone telling me exactly what to do and then standing over me to see that I did it. I suddenly realized that for the first time I was on my own. Everyone else had his own problems and no time to worry about mine. No one gave a damn what I did or how I did it.

It was a lonely feeling.

3.

The author as an Aviation Cadet with a Fairchild PT-19 primary trainer, Muskogee, Oklahoma. (Vincent Fagan collection)

I taxied out on my first mission with the Hot Rock's overload advice in the front and back of my mind.

While this was the first time I would be in combat, it was not the first time I was under fire. Just before graduation from cadets, the entire class was sent on a low altitude cross country flight. Northwest of Lawton, Oklahoma, I was skimming along fifty feet above the ground when I saw three large puffs of smoke about 100 yards in front of me. I wondered what they were and when I glanced to the left I knew.

We were flying across the gunnery range at Ft. Sill and there was a long row of cannons firing at us. The idiot that laid out the course programmed us to fly across the range. We were right on course and ultimately some two dozen AT-17's went streaking across the range. Which didn't faze the Army field artillery, they kept firing away and miraculously no one was hit.

I had never taken off a fully loaded B-24, much less one overloaded 10,000 lbs. But what the hell, for the first time I had 100 octane gasoline.

All I learned from the orientation flight was that the runway was too short, with too many chuck holes and too many olive trees at each end.

My experienced co-pilot turned out to be Bob Lang with 30 missions to his credit, though curiously, he had never taken off or landed a B-24. He was a nice guy and one hell of a formation pilot; shortly after this mission he got his own crew. I had a total of about 500 hours flying time, about 200 hours in a B-24. I sure wished I had more.

Joe Eagan's experienced co-pilot turned out to be on his second mission, so they could sort of learn together.

The target was Budapest, the Manfred Weiss Armament factory, on the banks of the Danube. I couldn't believe the briefing; it lasted all of five minutes. I was sure we'd get a milk run to Yugoslavia or Northern Italy. We were given a mimeographed sheet listing everything you needed to know. We were shown an aerial photo of the target, a few words from the intelligence officer, and a few words from the group

15

leader, and that was it.

We were to fly tail-end Charlie, number seven position, in No. 24, "Swamp Rat."

After the briefing, the crew and I were trucked out to the plane with a duffle bag of heavy clothing, a parachute, flak suit and Driggs, our bombardier, handed everyone an escape kit and a money pouch. He kept the morphine separate.

We stood around smoking cigarettes for a few minutes, pre-flighted the plane, the turrets, the radios and finally the yellow flare went up from the tower signalling "start engines."

We checked our engines, then got in a long line of planes taxiing out to the end of the runway. Finally it was our turn.

We got off the runway and cleared the olive trees with no difficulty. "Swamp Rat's" terminal illness was not takeoffs but gas consumption. We ran the race track pattern around the field, climbing, until we got into formation. At 10,000 feet, we started off to Budapest -- uphill all the way.

The struggle from the field to the target was to get some altitude to go over the target --- usually we left Frantic at 10,000 feet and went over the targets at an altitude of anything from 21,000 to 27,000 feet. Most targets were about 750 to 850 miles away and the round trip took about seven to eight hours.

We turned on the I.P. -- the initial point or starting point of the bomb run -- about 20 miles to the west of Budapest. We were last in the 15th Air Force -- the

16

twenty-first group to make the bomb run.

The sight ahead over Budapest was unbelievable -- the number of spent flak bursts must have numbered in the hundreds of thousands. I had seen flak movies, but this was 10 times the density I had ever seen. No movies or still photos I have ever seen have ever accurately represented what flak really looked like in the air. I don't know why.

We were still short of the flak area when six bursts of flak came up on my left. I looked out and the plane on my left, a hundred feet or so away, the number six man, was on fire between the fuselage and the #2 engine with a plume of flame reaching half way back to the tail assembly. The plane staggered along for about 3 or 4 seconds and then exploded. The gunners counted six chutes out. It was sickening.

If six bursts got one of us here, how in the hell were we ever going to get through what was up ahead. We were not permitted to do evasive action and I kept up as close as I could to the #4 man.

Bomb bay doors came open, then we sweated down the bomb run for about seven minutes.

"Bombs away."

The most beautiful words in the English language. We went into a screaming steep turn to the right and in about seven minutes we were in the clear. What a relief!

Then I got another shock.

I asked Rod East, the engineer, to give me a fuel reading; it turned out that we only had 350 to 400 gallons of gas left according to the fuel sight gauges. We had burned 2300 gallons on the way up and now we only had 400 gallons to get back. It didn't seem possible we could make it back with only that much gas even though we were descending instead of climbing.

The fuel sight gauges were two half inch glass tubes which theoretically showed the fuel level in the four main tanks by switching them back and forth. They were calibrated to show you the amount of gas in each tank, but the gas would jump up and down so much in the glass tubing so that you could only estimate within perhaps 100 gallons how much gas you had.

This was just one of the many pathetic features of a B-24 and there was no excuse for such a Mickey Mouse system, especially when gas was so critical most of the time. A B-24 costs about $450,000 and a few dollars spent for a decent fuel gauge or a fuel flow meter would seem like a sensible expenditure.

I cut the engines back to 2000 rpm and 27 inches -- but I didn't have much hope. However, we used only 200 gallons getting to the Adriatic.

We crossed over and hit the coast of Italy with less than 100 gallons showing. When we hit the field we peeled off, swung around in a 360 degree turn to the left and landed.

Just for curiosity sake I had Rod stay with the plane until it was refueled with gas to see how much gas we had left when we landed. The four gas tanks had a combined total of less than 50 gallons -- not enough to pull up and go around the field if you over-shot the runway. "Swamp Rat' eliminated itself from the scene shortly thereafter with some other unfortunate crew aboard.

A truck came out, we climbed in and were driven to the Red Cross doughnut stand. The nose gunner and waist gunner came up to me and announced that they were quitting. When asked why, they said they couldn't stand the sight of that plane blowing up on our left.

I knew "Fearless Red" wouldn't put up with this, but he did, and quit they did. I was glad to be rid of them. We got two new spare gunners from the pool.

Bob Felker was my co-pilot. He was a durable, easygoing Texan. He had spent almost his whole adult life flying. Today he operates a crop dusting service in Del Rio, Texas.

Bob didn't dislike the B-24 -- he loathed it. He went through cadets with the idea of being a fighter pilot -- destiny ruled otherwise. For a while, he acted as if he didn't pay any attention to the B-24, it would simply go away. It didn't. I used to plead with him to study up on the plane, dimensions, fuel transfer, location of fuse boxes and so forth.

The hell with it.

Finally, he got his own crew and with it a huge dose of reality.

He was unflappable, a very good formation pilot, very good under stress and saved my life on one occasion at

Vienna.
Hurray for Bob.

4.

An Italy-based 449th Bomb Group Liberator over Ploesti.

The second mission was Ploesti, with smoke up to 35,000 feet over the target; I couldn't believe it.

The plane behind me on take off went into the olive grove and blew up -- 5,000 pounds of bombs and 2,700 gallons of gas blew one guy's leg over a mile away in front of group headquarters. One plane blew up and another spun in over the target.

The third mission was Vienna -- on the bomb run I glanced out my side window just as the left wing of the plane alongside me was blown off by a direct hit. The plane flip-flopped down with no chutes out -- centrifugal force pins you in for the long minute or two to earth.

The fourth mission was to Athens and the fifth mission we went back to Budapest.

Our group lost 11 planes on these five missions, sending 28 each time. On this basis, using my handy pocket calculator/extrapolator it appeared that we could expect to get knocked down on our twelfth mission.

But it didn't work out that way. The odds got better the more missions you flew. If you got ten missions in you'd probably get forty -- not twelve.

We did not fly a permanently assigned plane. Every mission we were assigned a plane for that mission, usually a different one. I had been flying all the squadron junk for some time, "Swamp Rat", "Deuces Wild" (which flew sideways and couldn't be trimmed) and "Lucky Lady", which specialized in runway props and superchargers.

By my eighth mission, I had flown only one decent airplane, #339, "I'll Get By." Good engines, good instruments and radios and handled very well. One day I happened to be walking by the engineering shack and looked in and saw a list of planes on the wall. "What is the list for?" I asked a nearby corporal.

"Those are the planes in service for tomorrow. We call it over to Squadron operations at 4 o'clock every day."

"I'll Get By," #339 was on the list.

I went over to operations; if you were going to fly the next day your name went on the bulletin board at 3 p.m.

At 4 p.m. another list went up showing your position in the squadron box and the plane number you were to fly.

I told the corporal that my name was on the 3 p.m. list and would he please put me down for #339 which was coming over from engineering for the 4 p.m. list.

"Sure, no sweat."

Hallelujah! No more "Swamp Rat", "Deuces Wild", "Luck Ladies", etc. By the time I had flown 15 missions I had flown every plane in the squadron and knew which were the dogs. As a refinement, if some other crew flew #339, I had Rod, my engineer, check with the engineer of that crew after the mission while I checked with the pilot to make sure everything was O.K. We had two or three alternates, #059, #985 and #356 which were also excellent planes.

Oddly enough, new planes or planes with only a few missions were not necessarily the best planes to fly. No. 985 had 68 missions on it when it went down, and it was an excellent plane. Most planes lasted around 15 to 20 missions before they went down.

I told my friend, Joe Eagan, about my plane selection program and he adopted it also. We didn't discuss it with anyone else, and two custom planes per mission seemed enough of a strain on the plane pool. I noticed that most of my older friends seemed to be flying the same plane each mission also.

After the War, when I told this story to a friend of mine he thought it was the dirtiest, rottenest trick he had ever heard. Why should we have the best planes which left the new guys with the worst? I explained that we had the worst when we were new and besides a new man wouldn't know what plane to ask for until he'd flown them all. Also, no two pilots would necessarily agree on what was the best plane. I never did convince him, but I still think that under the circumstances what we did was not unfair.

It was a great psychological boost to think you had a good plane -- and flying the same plane over and over made you more familiar with its quirks and oddities.

I flew #339 'till it went down with another crew, then I switched to "Maiden America."

I spoke earlier about the pathetic fuel gauges. Some B-24s were equipped with Jack and Heintz flight indicators -- artificial horizons and directional gyros. Jack and Heintz had received tremendous publicity for the fantastic salaries they paid their employees.

There was only one thing wrong with their instruments -- they didn't work; and you could not fly in instrument conditions with them. The squadron ruled that any pilot assigned a plane with Jack and Heintz equipment could decline the mission if there was bad weather.

Whenever there was a crash near the field all the mechanics would race like hell to the scene to see if the plane had Sperry flight instruments that they could liberate and replace the diseased, high publicized Jack and Heintz dogs in their airplanes.

Another little dandy was the Sperry auto pilot; we were warned to be careful of it. When engaged, for no good reason, it would occasionally throw the plane into an outside loop. Since it was hydraulically activated it could not be overcome or disengaged before you peeled the wings off.

Having an auto pilot set up and ready to go like the Minneapolis Honeywell Electronic Unit was good insurance. Occasionally a control cable would be shot out -- you could fly the plane by engaging the auto pilot and flying it by way of the knobs on the auto pilot console. But you couldn't risk flying with the Sperry unit turned on.

5.

450th Bomb Group B-24s with post-Cottontails vertical stabilizer markings. (Vincent Fagan collection)

The Cottontails turned into the Black and Yellow tails. Or at any rate they seemed to.

When I got to the 450th Bomb Group, its nickname was the Cottontails and there was much evidence, in pictures and cartoons, that when they arrived in Italy, that all its planes' twin rudders were painted solid white.

Compared to the Pacific, the war in Europe was a pretty clean, chivalrous, Geneva-Convention type war. I know of no one who wouldn't rather be captured by the Germans than the Japanese.

Men in parachutes were never strafed although I wouldn't trust any flak gunners, and the custom arose that if you wanted to surrender, you simply dropped your landing gear to indicate that you were surrendering and your opponent would hold his fire until you could bail out with your crew.

The incident that is said to have caused the white painted tails to disappear, occurred when a 450th pilot with one engine out and straggling on the way home from the target was jumped by a lone Me-109. The Cottontail pilot told the crew to stay in the turrets; he dropped his gear and the Me-109 dropped flaps, slowed down, and pulled up alongside the crippled, surrendered B-24. The German pilot began to wave to the Americans with the expectation that they would begin jumping. The Cottontail pilot then ordered his gunners to open fire on the 109 and shot him down. This was easy to do under the circumstances.

The Cottontail pilot then pulled up his gear and went home.

That night, the Berlin Bitch, "Axis Sally," got on the radio and screamed bloody murder and at the end of her program gave the Cottontails 24 hours to get out of Italy.

On subsequent missions, German fighters ignored all other groups and singled out and attacked the Cottontails, knocking the daylights out of them. While breathing defiance, the Cottontails finally caved in and their tails, plus those of the 98th, 376th and 449th bomb groups -- all members of the 47th wing -- were painted yellow and black with slightly different cross hatching to distinguish each group, but similar enough to confuse Germans.

When I got to Italy the 450th had cross-hatched yellow and black tails.

Several things are unusual about this story. First, the identical story was told to me about an Eighth Air Force Group in England, and I heard it in the States before I ever went overseas. I was never able to find out if it was true or not.

Second, there were many officers and enlisted men with the 450th while I was there, who had come over with the original group when they were obviously Cottontails in design as in name. Yet, I never could pin any of them down about the truth of this story; about why the tails were changed from white to yellow and black. About all I got was evasion and double talk.

If I had to guess, I'd guess the story was true and if so I am opposed to the action the American pilot took. A fight to the finish is fine, but if you accept the blessings of chivalry you should be prepared to accept the obligations -- and the American pilot didn't.

Furthermore, he made life more difficult for later bomber crews who might have preferred to jump rather than have their heads blown off.

A further point; if an American officer has given his word that he is surrendering, and went back on it, the Army should straighten the matter out by turning him and his crew over to the Germans for imprisonment.

The Army reportedly did this in a similar circumstance that occurred in Switzerland.

An interned Eighth Air Force Officer is said to have given his parole that he would not escape if permitted to leave the Adelboden internment camp to get some eyeglasses in Zurich. Without telling the American Embassy that he had given his parole, they aided him in escaping to France and finally getting back to England.

When the Swiss protested, and proved they had his parole in writing, the Americans are said to have dumped him back in Switzerland, and rightly so I think.

World War II in the Pacific, and subsequent wars in Korea and Vietnam render the above ideas largely academic I think.

"Boobie Trap," a B-24H of the 450th Bomb Group with the original white "Cottontail" rudder markings.

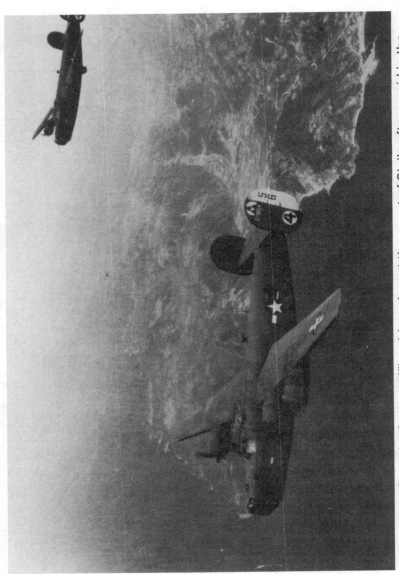

Two B-24Gs with "Cottontail" rudders depart the coast of Sicily after a raid in the spring of 1944.

"Maiden America," a B-24G-1 with the later black and yellow fin stripes over the Alps in the fall of 1944. This is the aircraft the author and his crew bailed out of following a raid on Innsbruck.

6.

Six crewmen died when the brakes of this 15th Air Force Liberator were accidentally applied on takeoff.

The bomb run was the worst part of a mission. But takeoffs were almost as bad.

The standard B-24 take off, as taught in the States, dictated that you slowly rolled onto the runway, slowly increasing power to 49 inches manifold pressure and 2700 R.P.M., maintaining directional control down the runway with rudder rather than brakes.

The engineer called air speed, the co-pilot watched the gauges and the pilot flew it. At 85 m.p.h. you pulled the nose wheel off the runway which put the plane in a climbing attitude and held it there till you reached 110 m.p.h. when it should start flying itself off the runway. Actually it bounced off and on three or four times and finally staggered into the air; as soon as you got off the runway, you brought the gear up, clear the trees, push the nose down and build air speed to 180 m.p.h. preparatory to climbing into formation.

The trouble with all this was that it didn't work very well in Italy. The planes were too overloaded, the runway too rough and short and the olive groves too close to the end of the runway. Usually about once a month someone went into the trees at the end of the runway, crashed and blew up on takeoff.

We took off in the dark at 2:00 a.m. for the invasion of Southern France. The first plane swung onto the runway and went tearing down to the other end, where it blew up. The #2 plane swung onto the runway, went roaring down the runway and also blew up at the other end.

The #3 plane did likewise. The plane in #4 position taxied back to the ramp, called the tower and asked if someone could check to see what the hell was wrong down at the end of the runway.

The tower called operations, who called Wing Headquarters to see if we could stand down until the end of the runway was checked.

Wing refused the request and told them to get going.

The #4 man taxied back -- let roll and made a normal takeoff. But when you got in the air you could see half a dozen planes from the other groups, sprinkled around the hell of the boot of Italy, burning on the ground. The sad part was that we got to the beaches too late to bomb.

I made several memorable contributions to the folk lore of crapped up takeoffs.

The first occurred when I had about five missions. I got off the runway at about 110 m.p.h. and headed for the olive trees. We heard the unusual loud "thunk" in the nose when we raised the nose wheel and it fell into the slot a little louder than usual.

We didn't think there was anything unusual about this and continued on the mission. When we returned and landed, about 100 mechanics and various sightseers walked out to meet us as we taxied onto the ramp.

I wondered what it was all about. I shut off the engines and climbed down through the bomb bay and out on the ramp to see what was wrong. The belly of the fuselage was ripped wide open from the nose turret to the front of the bomb bay about 12 inches deep and torn through the bulkheads and fuselage ribs.

When we heard the loud "thunk" on take off we had hit a four-inch diameter steel pipe, 50 feet high which was used as a runway marker light at night -- and knocked it flat to the ground. If we had hit it ten feet lower it would have slapped us in the face or ten feet to either side and it would have hit a prop and sent us cart-wheeling. I was offered a chance to go down and look at the pipe. In the interest of morale, I declined the offer.

Our second adventure came on a day when there was no headwind at all. Or as some wit would always say, the wind sock indicated that the wind was blowing straight down. This always made us feel bad; a good headwind got you off the ground and up and over the trees much quicker.

As we started to taxi onto the runway, I called out the final checklist.

"Booster pumps" -- "on"
"Mixture" -- "Auto Rich"
"Props" -- "Full High"
"Superchargers" -- "Set"
"Half Flaps" -- "Set"
"Cowl Flaps" -- "Coming Trail"

The plane felt all right as we came down the strip till we got halfway down the runway, from 35 m.p.h. on it felt sluggish, the engineer kept calling the air speed but he never got to 110 m.p.h., it just stuck at 105 m.p.h. We were too far committed to stop so I gave the wheel one hell of a yank. The plane staggered off the ground, wallowed around till it got up to 115 m.p.h. and finally we just barely cleared the trees.

And then the tail flutter started, until finally the entire fuselage was vibrating like hell. It immediately occurred to me that the plane was going to break up and fall apart in mid-air. I had never felt anything like this and it scared the hell out of me.

We were almost across the heel of the Italian boot, heading out to ditch in the ocean. If we couldn't make it back to the field I'd rather crash land than go into the water. There was not enough altitude for parachutes. I started to make a turn to the left; I glanced out to the left to clear myself for the turn and noticed the #1 and #2 engine nacelles.

33

Both cowl flaps were wide open -- a glance at #3 and #4 and they were likewise open. In effect we had taken off with our brakes on. This had caused all the buffeting and tail flutter and prevented our air speed from building up.

I turned to the co-pilot, Bob Felker, and as casually as possible asked him to please close the cowl flaps. He was supposed to have done this as we taxied out on the runway as part of the checklist. He got red in the face, looked at me, grinned and said, "Vince, I'll never sweat another takeoff as long as I live, if you can make it off with the cowl flaps open and no head wind." Neither of us were very happy about a no wind take off but a no wind take off with the cowl flaps open was unthinkable.

I don't know how or why we got away with it but I think it may explain the invasion of Southern France crashes and perhaps some of the one-a-month into the olive groves.

There were three things we needed to solve our take off problems:

1. Some concrete to cover our oiled dirt runway.

2. About 2,000 or 3,000 feet more runway.

3. A bulldozer to knock down the olive trees.

There was no chance of any of these things happening.

Joe Eagan, from Columbus, Ohio, was a great friend of mine. He provided the solution to the takeoff problem with his short field takeoff.

Joe ran the plane out on the runway, stopped, set the brakes and ran the engines up to 49 inches, 2700 r.p.m. He let it stay there for 4 or 5 seconds with the engines screaming like hell and the wings flapping up and down, then he snapped off the brakes. The plane would jump off down the runway, accelerate very quickly to 85 m.p.h., nose up and at 100 m.p.h. instead of letting it fly itself off, give it one big hellacious yank off the ground and keep it off until it wanted to fly.

I tried it and it worked great. Where I had been clearing the trees by five or ten feet before, I was now clearing them by fifty to seventy-five feet.

The only problem with this system was that the brass didn't like it. They wanted to see a plane rolling every 30 seconds on the runway on the theory that we could get into formation faster; but prop wash was scary as hell on takeoff and there was the possibility of the plane in front of you going into the trees and exploding just as you passed over it.

Major Hardin, Group Operations Officer, decided to get up in the tower and expedite things by screaming his head off at anybody who wasn't moving fast enough to suit him. He failed; too many pilots had reached the point where they'd do nothing they considered wrong.

When he'd scream at me, I'd just call him back and say: "Hello tower, this is ship in #1 position. Would you say again please, over." Then I'd go ahead with my short field runup and the hell with him. He finally gave up when Lt. Hal French called him back and said: "Goddammit Major, you fly the tower and I'll fly this goddam plane."

Several pilots stuck with the excess power approach to the problem -- they would run their engines up to 65 and

70 inches of manifold pressure which the turbo superchargers could produce and carry this power setting until they were clear of the trees. This was 40% over the red line, and could easily blow a cylinder head off, in which case you were dead.

I felt it was too risky and I continued to bounce around off the steel poles, olive trees, etc. until Eagan came along with his innovation.

7.

A B-24G-1 makes its approach. (Courtesy San Diego Aerospace Museum)

Dan King was one of the most engaging, talented persons I met while I was in the Army.

Dan was older than most of us, married and one of the few pilots who was old enough to have graduated from college. (I was 22 years old when I started flying combat and I would estimate the average pilot's age at 20 to 22 years old.) He was a Captain, a senior pilot with five years military flying experience and over 3,000 hours in a B-24. He was from Long Island, New York.

I first met him in Boise where, unlike many of the

tigers with a lot of instructional flying time, he took the time to go through Overseas Crew Training instead of going directly to a combat unit.

I got to know him better when he started the world's longest crap game in Lincoln, Nebraska and continued it aboard ship to Naples. He had a terrific song and dance routine, was great on impersonations and had a crew of characters who provided an excellent backdrop for his talents.

I thought he was a wonderful guy and one hell of a pilot -- his death really tore me up. It also raised the shattering question: if Dan couldn't stay alive with his experience and background, how in the hell was I going to do it?

Dan was leading the squadron to Vienna; with him as co-pilot he had Major Troost -- just over from the states with several thousand hours of B-24 instruction time on his first mission. On the way back from the target, as they crossed the Italian coast about 10 miles from the field, at 1500 feet altitude, Dan's #4 engine quit. The new major reached up and feathered #3 accidentally shutting off another engine.

At that altitude, with two engines out on one side there was no time to recover -- they smashed into the ground and burned. The only survivor was Major Troost, horribly burned, who confirmed what Joe Eagan had described from his #4 position in the squadron box.

When I heard about this I couldn't believe it -- I thought if anybody would finish his tour of 50 missions it would be Dan. It hit me so hard, I didn't even go to his funeral -- Joe Eagan and I started to go but decided we couldn't face it.

About three weeks later I was lying in the sack one afternoon when Corporal Cicero, the Squadron Operations Clerk, showed up with the news that I was to meet Major Bolt and his crew -- another hot shot instructor just in from the states -- and I was to go with them on an orientation flight over to the gunner range.

My mind was on Dan King and his major as I started out to the flight line. I introduced myself to Major Bolt who was standing about 100 feet from his crew. The Major was a bright-eyed, handsome individual.

"Well, shall we go," he inquired pleasantly.

He seemed like a nice guy -- and I felt that right now was probably the high water mark of our relationship.

"Wait a minute, Major, before we get in the airplane there's one thing you have to know," I said.

"What's that," he asked.

"You can fly the airplane, but if anything goes wrong, it has to be understood that I am in command of the airplane." I said.

His face dropped, he just looked at me in surprise, he couldn't seem to comprehend what I had said; First Lieutenants just didn't talk to Majors that way. After a pause he said:

"Do you realize I have 3,000 hours in a B-24?"

"Yes Major, but I've got 31 combat missions -- how many do you have?"

He paused again -- he couldn't believe it, but he seemed to be getting the message that I meant what I was saying.

All I had to do was double up with a stomach ache and good old Captain Jones, Squadron Flight Surgeon, would be happy to ground me for the rest of the day -- as long as I didn't miss any combat missions.

"Look Major, " I said, "nobody has to know what the deal is: I'll sit in the co-pilot seat, I'll call the checklist, pull up the gear and flaps -- no one on your crew has to know what the arrangement is. But if anything goes sour, I run things."

The Major looked very unhappy, red in the face, but he finally bought it. There was not much else he could do.

We got in the plane with his crew standing on the flight deck behind us. We went through the checklist, taxied out, and then went screaming down the runway with the Major at the controls. We got off the ground and when we got about 200 feet in the air, at 120 m.p.h. -- 10 m.p.h. above stalling speed -- the Major racked it over in a 45 degree bank.

I reached over, hit him in the chest and hollered, "I got it." I rolled it out level, dropped the nose, gear up and flaps up. When I got it up to 180 m.p.h., I started climbing out till I reached 5,000 feet. I then gave it back to the Major and indicated the direction to the gunnery range.

He took over with a sheepish grin on his face and said, "What's the matter? What did I do wrong?"

"Major," I said, "you are going to find that you are going to get enough thrills over here without doing 45 degree banks on takeoff."

"Oh that," he laughed, "I did that all the time back in the states."

"Major, you can do it over here all the time too -- just as soon as I get the hell out of this plane," I responded.

He didn't ask me any questions about my prejudice against chandelles off the runway, so I didn't tell him anything. I didn't tell him about the overload situation, about load adjustment/weights and balance, about how to get his hooks on a good plane, or any number of facts that would help him stay alive. We were simply light years apart on our plans for survival.

Perhaps I would not have taken the same strong stand with him if Dan had not recently had his experience with his Major or if the hot rock had not warned me about these types that first night in the Officer's Club Bar.

While he was trying to overwhelm me with his 3,000 hours flying time in a B-24, I had correctly replied that they weren't combat hours and in effect he was comparing apples and oranges.

He could fly circles around me in a 35,000 pound stripped-down B-24 but we were flying a 70,000 pound airplane. He had no flying time in this beast, while I had specialized in it for some time.

My recollection is, that the good Major got six missions in before he went down. He apparently hadn't wasted much time talking to other pilots about this airplane either.

8.

I hated fires in planes.

Even when they were started by my old buddy, Ned Glover from Los Angeles, the friendliest, most likable guy I ever met, and an excellent pilot.

Unfortunately, he was also the unluckiest guy I ever met. He was always in hot water from foul ups not of his making. He had a certain deft touch for getting into various jams; you might say he had the Midas touch -- everything he touched turned to shit.

The night before he was to be married, he very carefully avoided the bachelor party thrown for him by some friends so that he wouldn't be hung over for his wedding. Instead he went out with a friend for dinner and when he started for home at 9:00 p.m., he slipped and fell in a gravel drive way leaving his face cut up almost beyond recognition.

When he showed up at the church, cut, bruised and bandaged, it looked as if he had been on one hell of a bender when the reverse was true. This was a typical Ned Glover operation.

The first time I flew with him the gear would go down and visually lock but the red light would stay on and the horn would blow, indicating it was not locked and would collapse upon landing.

After fooling around for an hour to correct it, getting the meat wagons and fire trucks all stirred up, we finally landed and found out the light and horn were wrong.

Ned's fire came about in the following manner. We were making an instrument check in a twin engine C47, the military counterpart of the DC3.

Captain Walters, the check pilot was sitting in the right hand seat, I was flying under the hood in the left seat, and Ned was standing between the seats.

Suddenly, he nudged the check pilot, Captain Walters, and said: "Say Captain, what's under the floor boards down there," indicating the area on which he was standing.

Captain Walters turned in his seat, looked down, and said, "Oh, there's gasoline booster pumps, hydraulic pumps and gas lines. Why?"

"Well, I just dropped a cigarette on the floor and when I went to step on it, it rolled into that hole under the floor boards," said Ned.

We were within sight of the field, I called Frantic Tower, "Hello Frantic, this is Army #972. We are about 5 miles south of the field, I am starting a turn to the left. Would you please put the binoculars on us and see if we are smoking or if we are on fire."

"Negative, #972," from the tower.

"We are going to make a straight-in approach, as we have a possible fire on board. Would you please keep the glasses on us and let us know if we start showing smoke or have any flames. Also, would you please alert the fire trucks and meat wagons," I said.

"Roger #972," from the tower.

We had chutes and could have jumped, which might have proved embarrassing if the plane didn't subsequently burn when it hit the ground. The real danger would come on the final approach when we got below 1000 feet -- we would then be too low to jump and would have to land or attempt a landing no matter what kind of fire broke out. All the way down the final approach, I was sure I could smell smoke. And my seat felt warmer.

We landed, to the escort of the fire trucks and ambulances, tore up the floor boards and never did find Ned's cigarette.

9.

The letter from Dan Driggs, my bombardier, said that they were going to break up my crew and reassign each of them to some other crew.

Dan wrote to me at the Army hospital in Bari where I'd been for six weeks with amoebic dysentery. In all that time I had actually talked to a doctor twice, for about a total of 15 minutes.

I had lain there in this ward and done nothing all this time; the only entertainment we had was from an alcoholic chaplain who was in the ward with us. He was drunk almost all the time. He was a Southern hell-fire and damnation revivalist, he sang, told jokes, made speeches and was a great enlivening influence.

If I lost my crew, it meant they'd build a new one for me when I got back out of all the misfits, halfwits and meat heads they could scrape together. I simply could not let that happen no matter what.

If I was going to hang on to my crew, I had to get back to the bomb group today, 100 miles away. I had no transportation but I could hitch hike. The tricky part was to get out of the hospital before the medics could stop me. I got out of bed, put on my clothes and started packing my B-4 bag.

In walked Nurse Fletcher -- Lt. Fletcher: "What the hell do you think you're doing, Fagan?"

"I'm going back to my bomb group," I replied.

"You are doing no such thing," she said, "get back in the bed immediately."

"I told you, I'm going back to my bomb group," I replied.

"I am giving you a direct order to get back in that bed," she screamed.

"I am going back to my bomb group."

"I'll go get Captain Henderson, he'll fix you," she said and rushed out of the ward.

I was finishing packing when Captain Henderson arrived with Lt. Fletcher in tow.

"Lt. Fagan," said the Captain. "I am giving you a direct order to get back in that bed."

"I am going back to the bomb group," I said finishing zipping up my B-4 bag and walking toward the door.

"Lt. Fagan, you are going AWOL and I am going to have you court martialed," he said trailing after me.

I turned around and faced him, "Captain," I said, "they court martial you for running away from combat -- not for running towards it."

I turned and walked out of the hospital and no one attempted to stop me.

In theory of course, Henderson could really lower the boom on me. But I felt that if I could get back to the bomb group before the medics caught up with me, it would be impossible to make any A.W.O.L. charge stick.

46

Besides I felt that the Bomb Group would move to protect me once I got back. They could always flange up some kind of story to get these people off my back. The bomb group management was definitely prejudiced toward people who wanted to fly missions as opposed to someone who was sacked out in a hospital ward.

I hitch hiked back to Frantic, went into the Squadron operations office and told Corporal Cicero that I was out of the hospital and ready to fly. He said fine, he'd put my crew up for the next day's mission and that was that.

The crew was glad to see me back, it meant they'd get more missions in, they could fly as a unit and would not be transferred individually to a strange crew.

What is puzzling about this affair, is that after I came back to the bomb group, no one in any administrative capacity ever said a word to me about it. No one ever asked how I got out of the hospital, how I got back to the group, if I was officially discharged, where were my orders, my 201 file -- nothing.

How it was handled from a record keeping standpoint, I don't know. I wouldn't be surprised if the 450th simply denied that I ever came back. As long as you were flying your missions, showing up faithfully and on time to fly and not making any early returns, "Fearless Red" and company wouldn't let anyone hassle you.

At any rate, I am still officially A.W.O.L. from the Twenty-Sixth General Hospital in Bari.

After the war I discussed this with an Air Force Top Sergeant. He said the solution to the mystery was very simple. The hospital people simply said the hell with it, if he'd rather fly than be in the hospital, mark him "returned to duty" send his papers back and forget it.

10.

Burma Bound, a 451st Bomb Groub Liberator, one down and three to go after Munich raid. (Courtesy San Diego Aerospace Museum)

Having all four engines quit simultaneously over the target, happened only once as far as I know. This remarkable incident and subsequent recovery happened to Bob Woodlin and he told me the story in Naples on our way home.

Bob was a professional baseball player and we went through cadets together but we finally got separated after going through B-24 Pilot Transition, though we both wound up in Italy.

49

He was on a mission somewhere in Northern Italy, south of the Alps around Udine. Bob was leading a seven ship box and he led the bomb run down to the target. Over the target, just as the bombs went away, he was bracketed by a half dozen burst of flak and all four engines quit simultaneously.

He was at 27,000 feet and started losing 5,000 feet per minute. Bob jumped on the engines with every emergency procedure he ever heard of. He finally got two engines going when he was down to about 15,000 feet. He called the navigator down in the nose for a heading to an airfield across the front lines.

No response.

The navigator, bombardier and nose gunner had bailed out over the target. Which wasn't an act of cowardice -- every crew member had the right to jump anytime he thought the situation required it.

Bob headed south with the co-pilot navigating and losing altitude all the way. They crossed the front lines at 10,000 feet. Shortly after they hit 5,000 feet they picked up a P-38 fighter plane escort who slowed down and flew alongside Bob. Bob and he started talking on the radio and the fighter pilot told him that there was a fighter field a few miles ahead.

By the time they got within sight of the field and set up for a final approach, Bob started to drop the landing gear and flaps when one of his remaining engines quit. Bob hollered to the men in the tail to bail out and the co-pilot scrambled out ahead of him.

By the time Bob climbed out of his seat they were

down to 800 feet; when Bob got to the bomb bay, the bomb bay door was cracked open about two feet wide. Rather than climb the three feet down into the bomb bay, Bob dove from the flight deck through the opening in the bomb bay. He got out of the plane but his back chute wedged inside the bomb bay between the bomb bay door and the cat walk.

He was below 500 feet and struggling wildly to free himself. At 250 feet he broke loose, snapped his rip cord, the chute opened and he swung once and hit the ground leaving some very deep foot prints. The P-38 buzzed him and waved - calling ahead to the fighter strip to send a truck out to pick up Bob. It was a great mission to walk away from.

11.

There was not much to do the night before a mission --
but then there was not much to do even if there was no
mission.

I didn't like to go to the movies -- usually I started
running emergency procedures through my head, like if
you lose #3 engine, you lose the hydraulic pump, so you
have to let the wheels down manually and you only have
one shot at the brakes before you exhaust the
accumulators -- and couldn't keep track of the movie
plot which usually wasn't much anyway.

We were too far off the beaten track for the live Bob
Hope-type U.S.O. entertainers, though Bebe Daniels
and Ben Lyon came out of retirement from England to
grace, live, our modest stage.

The long distance, super marathon, gigantic Poker
Game was always on at the Officer's Club. This was for
previous big winners and a half dozen or so players were
in more or less constant attendance; it was not at all
unusual for the winner to walk out with $5,000 for his
night's work.

The shipboard crap game which started in Omaha and
continued to Naples, stopped there never to go again. I

never saw a crap game in Italy.

The bridge game was for fun rather than for keeps and I occasionally played with Cargill, the bombardier, who worked his way through Notre Dame playing bridge. After you saw him play, you might as well play for fun rather than money. He never lost.

You could get a drink at the bar but there was almost no drinking at Frantic. A few guys would trade in a warm beer for a cold one and that was about it. While there was plenty of booze about, there was almost no drinking and I never could figure out why.

During the thirties, I used to see various World War I flying movies usually featuring Errol Flynn and David Niven who, returning from a flight, would stamp into the bar in the old chateau, bemoan the loss of a good old Joe, bottoms up with the cognac and fling the empty glass into the fireplace across the room.

Errol and David must have eaten better than we did. Our first maneuver on landing was to get the hell over to the Red Cross doughnut stand and get some coffee and doughnuts, the best food available. We usually flew without breakfast or lunch.

The flight surgeon issued each crew member two ounces of 100 proof Old Overholt rye after each mission. A searing jolt to an empty stomach that everyone passed up after the first time. I established the practice of collecting the 20 ounces due our crew after each mission and any crew member could later take what he wanted.

In addition, the Officers were issued one fifth of Schenley Green Label per month. At one time, I had 18 fifths of whiskey in my house and no takers.

As far as drinking was concerned, I was in the wrong war.

12.

"Bombs Away". Photo by tail gunner in the Italy-based 449th Bomb Group. The Mairhoff bridge was the target. The forbidding Alps range on both sides of the formation.

Talking about flying, reading paperbacks and sack time were the one, two, three preferred non-flying activities.

No one went to town at night. Manduria was placid enough in the daytime with M.P.s patrolling it: at night it was no place to be. My nose gunner, Olean, inadvertently got caught out at night and wound up in the hospital, beat up and cut badly. Viva Il Duce!

Dan Driggs and I learned this same lesson painlessly within 48 hours of arriving in Naples. We wandered away from the Repple Depot late in the afternoon and wound up after nightfall drinking vino with some convivial Italianos.

When we tried to find our way home, on a pitch dark night, we found ourselves hopelessly lost. Ahead of us we finally saw four American soldiers and decided to follow them for want of any better plan. They led us down a dark alley and suddenly we found ourselves the object of several flashlights and four .45 caliber automatics.

They wanted to know why the hell we were following them. I told them that I was an Army pilot and Dan my bombardier and we were lost. Oh boy! wonderful -- they thought we were M.P.s and were ready to shoot us since they were A.W.O.L. They were with the 101st Airborne, knew where the Repple depot was and would be happy to take us back there, which they did, through the back door, so to speak.

I would have hated to have been around if any M.P.s showed up, but none did and that ended any future wandering around in the dark in Italy.

I usually went to bed around 11:00 p.m. They'd wake you up at 4:30 a.m. -- usually the briefing was at 5:30 or 6:00 a.m. and start engines at 6:45 a.m. with takeoff at 7:00 a.m.

You simply couldn't sleep in the barracks. Some idiot would come stumbling through every half hour, kicking over various cigarette cans, waste baskets, etc. You could hope for only a few good hours sleep, which didn't matter -- I never saw anyone get sleepy on a mission.

When we built our house, we finally managed to get four or five hours sleep a night.

In theory, when you got up at 4:30 a.m. you were supposed to go to breakfast. I never did. I couldn't face the alternative of fried C rations or peanut butter sandwiches and the mess hall was a mile walk. I didn't think it was worth it.

Usually most of the guys slept another half hour. I found this an excellent time to work out with the unpredictable shower facilities. There were two showers for 600 men which was discouraging but generally they were accessible at 4:30 in the morning and wonder of wonders there was hot water.

There was usually a line waiting to get into the briefing room and when the guy in front of you saw the red line on the map leading to the target, you'd hear "Jesus Christ". Up till then you'd be absolutely certain that *today* it was going to be a milk run.

King Zog's Palace in Tirana, Albania was always the most-mentioned, ideal mission. Vienna or Ploesti and King Zog's Palace were light years apart in danger and difficulty.

Mimeographed sheets were handed out giving all the radio recognition signals which nobody used, takeoff time, various other oddments of information such as courses, check points and turn points, I.P. (Initial Point: start of the bomb run), time to meet fighter escort, etc.

After a few missions you learned not to pay much attention to all this meticulous planning. It was rare that you ever met up with the other bomb groups and sometimes you went all the way to the target with just the seven planes in your squadron without meeting up with any other planes as you were supposed to.

The Intelligence Officer usually put some pictures of the actual target on a screen and then gave a two or three minute dissertation on why the target must be destroyed. It was my opinion that Intelligence Officers were the characters who were the furthest removed from reality of anyone in the combat situation.

One day when we were going to Munich, the Intelligence Officer advised us that if we got shot down over Munich, to walk south to the Alps, work our way through the Alps to Northern Italy and seek help from friendly Italian partisans behind German lines.

Can't you just picture a young, well-fed, rosy-cheeked American in flying clothes, who can't speak German, with no German money, no way to buy food, no way to read road signs, no way to ask directions "working his way through the Alps" with a completely hostile citizenry aligned against him?

Or as another advised, if we got shot down over Vienna, we were to follow street car line #111 out to the edge of town to a slave labor camp where the inmates were sympathetic and would assist you.

Presumably, after you went swaggering through Vienna in an American uniform, unable to speak German, unable to read any signs, to a slave labor camp with no guards to detect you, you would have no difficulty breaking into the slave labor camp to seek help from the friendly slaves, who, of course, couldn't help themselves.

Anyone who advised you to "work your way through the Alps" just hasn't seen the Alps.

I didn't waste much time listening to such exotic advice. Americans who escaped from France, Yugo, and Northern Italy did so because some dedicated native picked them up, hid them, fed them and moved them along the underground Partisan railroad.

Virtually no American escaped from Germany, Austria, Hungary, Rumania, Czechoslovakia or Bulgaria. The first requisite for escape was a friendly populace and the ability to speak the language.

I must insert one or two intelligence triumphs to counter-balance their insane recommendations on how to escape from Germany.

We took pictures, bomb strike photos as they were called, at the time we dropped our bombs, though if the target was overcast no pictures were possible.

As soon as clear weather prevailed over various targets, stripped-down P-38's were dispatched at 38,000 and 40,000 feet, to check on what rebuilding progress was being made. This was high enough and fast enough (400 plus m.p.h.) that nothing could get at them.

I was frequently puzzled when I first started flying, that someone in the group would call out that there were German fighters in the area and to tighten up the formation. I couldn't figure out how this information was obtained. I'd look around and could see no fighters or vapor trails to indicate fighters, and I always wondered how someone was able to tell that there were German fighters in the area.

Later, when Driggs and I finished building our house, I met what looked like a couple of German enlisted men who lived across the street from us. They spoke English with a German accent but obviously learned German first. They both said they were children of immigrants and were radio operators, though they belonged to no crew and kept very much to themselves.

One day I flew a plane for the first time and here was one of the German radio operators aboard. But the radio he was operating was not the standard B-24 long range AM radio.

I asked him what was going on.

He grinned and said I'd figure it out anyway. The Americans had broken the German fighter/controllers code and both he and his friend were from the Vienna area and spoke various German/Austrian dialects in the area we flew.

They monitored the German fighter controllers commands and could tell where the fighters were and how close they were to our group. When they got within about five minutes of us he'd call me on the intercom and let me know and I could alert the rest of the group. Beat the hell out of squinting into the sun all day.

The briefing was very short -- usually less than ten minutes. After the usual pie-in-the-sky advice from the Intelligence Officer, the Group Leader would get up with the permanent request to keep the formation in close and for Christ's sake don't straggle. And that was it -- no careful scrutiny by the Flight Surgeon, no solemn prayer by the Chaplain.

60

We were issued our flak helmets and flak suits, Driggs distributed an escape kit (compass, maps, benzedrine, halazone tablets, sulfa tablets, and forty-eight American dollars) to each crew member while he hung on to about a dozen morphine styrettes.

All this went onto a truck with your heavy clothing and parachute, and the entire crew was delivered to the plane you were going to use for the day.

13.

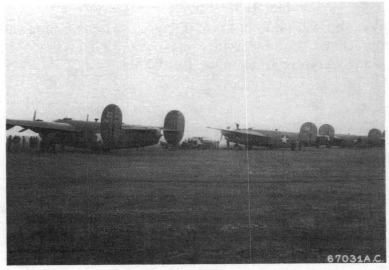

The 396th Bomb Group at Benghazi, Libya after an early Ploesti raid.

Originally, all air crews were issued sheepskin/wool flying clothes which were very warm but which were so air tight they caused you to sweat and then you would freeze when you got to altitude.

We used cotton suits with synthetic fur and a plug-in electric suit underneath. These breathed and were quite comfortable at even minus 30 or 40 degrees.

The big decision was shoes.   We were issued

electrically heated boots made of felt which kept your feet very warm but they were hell to walk out of Yugoslavia with. The alternative was G.I. shoes and sheepskin-lined heavy boots which kept your feet molto cold. A permanent frostbite candidate but you could walk out of Yugoslavia if you went down. A hell of an answer but you had to make the decision.

Bob Crowe, my navigator, went on a night intruder mission with another crew, got frostbite in his feet and wound up having both his feet amputated as a consequence.

After spending a few minutes preflighting the plane, the crew usually stood around smoking cigarettes, waiting the five or ten minutes to start-engine time.

About once a month, the crew would be flattened by a burst of machine gun fire as some gunner checked his guns and turret and accidentally let loose a blast with twin .50 caliber bullets. In theory, this couldn't happen because of various safety devises, but this happened quite often; no one was ever hit. Sure scared the hell out of you though.

The worst experience prior to take off happened not to me but to our squadron armament officer, Lt. George Ford.

We had been dropping delayed action bombs at Vienna which were set to go off between six and 36 hours after we dropped them. We dropped leaflets with these bombs advising the German workers that there were delayed action bombs covered by rubble in their plant area and that it would be prudent to stay away from work for about a week. Unfortunately, German demolition teams jumped in and immediately diffused our delayed action bombs.

We then introduced our new booby trap fuse. It was designed so that if anyone attempted to remove it from the bomb it would automatically detonate the bomb if it were turned counter-clockwise one fourth turn.

Most people, when they start turning a threaded fitting and it sticks, almost always involuntarily reverse the process. Since this, of course, would blow up the plane and all nearby, it was decided to let only the squadron Ordnance Officer insert the booby trap fuses.

We were supposed to stand back while Lt. Ford screwed in the dangerous fuse.

I watched him from about 200 feet -- hardly a safe distance -- and after about five minutes I wondered what had gone wrong, he was standing motionless, bent over the bomb bay.

I walked up to him and asked him what was wrong. Sweat was pouring down his face, he had started a fuse but it didn't go in even an eight of a turn when the threads blocked -- no one had told him what to do in this situation. He didn't dare back off the fuse for fear it would explode, he couldn't be sure if he let go if it would fall out of the bomb and detonate it.

He asked me to go get him some tape -- he then taped the fuse to the bomb, the plane was later flown out over the Mediterranean and the bomb dropped in the water. We took a spare plane.

Bombs were normally very safe to handle. In theory at

least, you can hit one with a sledge hammer and it will not detonate if it doesn't have a fuse.

Even with a fuse, there are several safety devices involved that prevent accidental detonation. There is a small wind vane attached to the fuse that must spin through an air drop of several hundred feet before the fuse, and therefore the bomb, is armed. In addition, there is a cotter pin in the wind vane which prevents the vane from spinning and arming the bomb accidentally until the pin is pulled.

Several times I saw planes land with a bomb hung up in the rack. Normally, these things were chopped out with an axe over enemy territory but occasionally you couldn't get them out. No matter how smooth the landing, they would break loose, tear through the bomb bay door and go tumbling end over end down the runway at 100 m.p.h. I saw this happen several times and the bomb did not explode, the fuse having been removed.

14.

Hydraulics out, this 304th Bomb Wing Liberator used crew parachutes to slow its landing at a base in Italy.

Engine start up, which is signalled by a flare fired from the tower, is the last time you secretly hope the mission will be called off. Particularly if it is Ploesti, Munich, Vienna or some other flak trap. Occasionally you get up in the morning with the premonition that this your day to get clobbered and if the feeling is strong enough, cancellation is a welcome thing. But after you start your engines, you have too much time and emotion invested to make it worthwhile to cancel.

Driggs, Rod, Bob Felker and I all started the engines together. If we didn't all agree that the gauges read right, we'd dump the plane, call for a truck and move over to a spare which was always kept running for just such situations.

We'd always call in the crew chief and show him why we were turning down the plane. This frequently resulted in arguments by this personage that our objections didn't justify turning down the plane. I would simply tell him that in my opinion #3 engine had too much mag drop and ask Driggs, Rod and Bob if they agreed. When they did, we would shut off the engines and move on to the spare.

There simply was no sense in going off on a mission in a plane that was mechanically below par. Even if it were perfect, some things would go sour on the way that we would have to contend with. The problem the crew chief faced was mainly one of pride. He had reported the plane ready to the engineering officer and now we had contradicted him.

An unfair and overwhelming argument (and one I never used) was to tell the crew chief to get a parachute and come along.

According to regulations, no pilot even had to make a rational statement about an airplane in refusing to fly it; he could say he simply did not feel right about the plane and refuse to fly it. No one could override his judgment (although they might make life miserable for him as a result of his judgment).

The simplest way to stop the controversy was to go get in another plane and fly the mission in it.

But, the same rules applied to the second plane; if it was no good, dump it. I once turned down three airplanes in a row and finally went off in the fourth plane which was the first plane I had turned down which, in the meantime, had been fixed.

Which warrants a discussion here of mission credits and early returns or aborts, as they were known in the 8th Air Force.

It becomes apparent that if you have a mission to bomb a lonely bridge in Yugoslavia, everyone wants to go. If you have a mission to Ploesti or Vienna or Berlin, the three roughest targets in Europe, no one wants to go.

Some equalizers had to be introduced into the situation. Originally, the mission formula was based on an approximate 4% loss ratio per mission in the Eighth Air Force in England, so that if you completed 25 missions in heavy bombers, you could go home. In theory you should have been shot down after 25 missions and since you had managed to beat the odds you had fulfilled your mission flying obligations.

However, when part of the Eighth Air Force was moved to North Africa, because of the shorter missions and easier targets, the figure of 50 missions was used for the completion of a tour.

When the African units were moved up to Italy, primarily to go after the Axis oil at Ploesti and Vienna, both the 50 mission and 25 mission theories were invoked.

You had to fly 50 missions to complete a tour but the big rough targets gave you double mission credit -- Ploesti, Vienna, Munich, Budapest and the like. For anything else you got a single mission credit.

Also, in theory, if you turned back short of the target and returned early to base, the pilot got an automatic fine of $75. There was an early return board meeting, consisting of the pilot, co-pilot, flight engineer, ground crew chief, engineering officer, and Squadron Commander.

Someone was supposed to catch hell, but it never happened -- it was something like combat fatigue which wasn't supposed to happen.

There were several characters who were professional early return artists -- one of these, after being in the group for over a year had less than five missions. I once got more missions than that in a week.

Maybe you could outwit the numbers this way but I thought it was stupid. These guys usually took off and went out on course for a while till the expected malfunction erupted (low on oxygen was very popular) then they turned around and went back, dropping their bombs enroute in the Adriatic.

They went through the risk of a take off and landing and part of the trip to the target and were no closer to terminating their exposure to risk by finishing their tour than when they started.

I felt that once you made a takeoff you sure as hell were committed to a landing and with a little on course flying you had taken on almost half the risk of a mission, why settle for less than a mission credit?

Frequently, it was safer to continue on, staying in the bomber-fighter stream even if you could not keep up with your group, than turning back and returning to the base alone, a sitting duck for a lone wandering enemy fighter.

15.

Bottoms Up, a lonely 450th Bomb Group B-24 in its early Cottontails markings makes its way over water back to Manduria, Italy. (Courtesy San Diego Aerospace Museum)

We were on our way to Vienna one day when we lost our #3 supercharger which at 20,000 feet was equivalent to losing the engine. We rapidly fell back from the group.

We were over Austria and I called Dan Driggs and asked him if there was anything to bomb ahead of us. He said there was the little town of Waldheim about three minutes ahead. I called the navigator and asked him to look up the town of Waldheim on the flak charts. "No flak," he replied.

Dan called and said he had the pins pulled, bomb bay doors coming open, and for me to center and follow the P.D.I., meaning he would be flying the ship through the bomb sight.

We made one hell of a short bomb run, and Driggs got 5,000 pounds of bombs on Waldheim, when all hell broke loose from below in the form of a startling inaccuracy of the flak chart.

What could have been so valuable in this little town to warrant all the flak they put up, I never did find out. We got the hell out of there.

We were to the west of Vienna, the lead groups had bombed Vienna thirty minutes earlier and rallied north and circled around Bratislava. If we headed east we should be able to meet the lead groups and stay in the bomber/fighter stream all the way back, even with only three engines.

It was a ticklish navigation job. There was a solid undercast below us when we got to Vienna. We went between Vienna and Weiner Neustadt and picked up the turn point for the course home. We threaded our way between the two towns with flak coming up on both sides but no hits.

No fighters or bombers had yet arrived at the turn point. There was no particular apprehension however, we were 500 feet above the undercast, if we got hit by fighters we could simply drop into the soup and lose them; when we got farther down the line in Yugoslavia at a lower altitude we would pick up the use of our #3 engine.

We broke out at Split, Yugoslavia and proceeded on back to Frantic gallantly leading the entire Air Force which never did catch up with us.

We landed and checked the plane -- over 50 flak holes administered by the helpless little town of Waldheim. We received more damage than any other plane in the squadron that day and got two mission credits.

While there was some danger from fighters flying the hundred miles alone over to the Vienna/Bratislava turn point, as opposed to simply turning around and going back before Waldheim, which would have returned no mission credit, yet it would have posed about as much risk.

If we had decided on an early return we would have come home worn out and empty handed. My entire crew agreed with me on this policy -- once we taxied out and took off we wanted a mission credit and would do whatever it took to get a mission credit.

We constantly looked for reasons to go rather than stay. We were taxiing out to take off on a mission to Sjenica, Yugoslavia, to bomb a bridge. It seemed so easy, the way it was presented at the briefing, that I would have taken off for it on three engines if possible. Our nose gunner, Olean, had not shown up that morning so we had only an eight man crew.

As we started to taxi out for takeoff, our good Corporal Cicero, El Supremo of the Operations Office, came racing alongside in a Jeep wildly flagging us down. We stopped and he hastened up through the bomb bay to the flight deck.

"What's the trouble," I asked.

"You can't go on the mission; you've only got eight crew members," he said.

"There's no law that says I can't fly with only eight men," I stated.

He blinked, trying to think of some other argument. He found it.

"Well, you can't fly a mission without a nose gunner and you haven't got one," he said triumphantly.

"I certainly have, Dan Driggs here is a qualified nose gunner, aren't you Dan?" I said.

"I sure am," Dan replied, which made him navigator, bombardier, and nose gunner for the mission.

Crestfallen, Corporal Cicero withdrew. He had survived so many operations officers that he thought of himself as Squadron Operations' permanent manager. Which he was, and the kindest thing he was ever called was "shit head".

I never did ask Dan if he could operate a nose turret. It really didn't make any difference. The idea of him sitting in the nose turret with his maps and dividers spread on his lap while clutching the bomb toggle switch in his hot little hand, is of course, absurd.

What matters is that we got Corporal Cicero out of the way and went on the mission as planned.

Driggs, our bombardier, was an aristocrat, an Ivy League graduate and at twenty-seven well past middle age as air crewmen went.

But he was a tough minded, determined individual who could be counted on to make the correct response no matter what the situation.

By trade he was a bombardier, yet in performance he was about the best navigator I ever saw and he spent most of his flight time navigating.

He was one of the best friends I had in the Army and he still occupies that position thirty odd years later.

16.

A four engine airplane is a large device that screws holes in the air. This is generally called prop wash and is a form of violent localized turbulence.

If you get behind a B-24 in the air, your plane jumps all over the place, no matter what you do to control it, the plane bucks, jerks, and jumps beyond any control -- you simply have no control over your airplane, till you get out of the stuff.

Usually, this kind of prop wash is encountered on the runway when making a takeoff.

When making the race track pattern and climbing to altitude, frequently a box leader would drag you through another box's prop wash. The prop wash from a seven ship box simply cannot be imagined, hardly described.

The B-24 is a large heavy piece of equipment and it would go completely out of control like an insane bucking bronco. No matter what you did, jump on the rudder, cross control, full aileron left, right, full throttle, low r.p.m., high r.p.m., full flaps; nothing worked, you were all over the sky and the guys in formation alongside you were in the same boat. How mid-air collisions were avoided, no one knew.

The only way to straighten out the mess was to get on the radio and scream your head off at the idiot box leader who dragged you into all this crap. When the squadron leader would finally get it through his head what was going wrong he would pull up or pull out and stop the pain.

I never saw a mid-air collision from prop wash but I don't know why -- it was vicious stuff.

17.

Whoever dreamed up the idea of daylight precision bombing must have predicated all his ideas on the concept of permanent universal C.A.V.U. (ceiling and visibility unlimited) weather.

Unfortunately, we almost never saw any of this. Even in the summer, large billowing cumulo-syphilis clouds blocked the way to the target. In the winter, there were more of them laterally than vertically.

The Air Corps solved the weather problem very easily. They pretended it didn't exist. In addition to not paying any attention to what the Intelligence Officer had to say at the briefing, I began to not pay any attention to what the meteorology genius had to say at the briefing either.

It would be raining like hell with the ceiling at about two hundred feet, so he would come on with, "The ceiling is scattered and broken at about 1,000 feet and you will break out on top at about 2,500 feet."

When you got off and into the crap you'd finally break out on top at about 10,000 -- but you'd never go back to discuss this with the metro man -- you might as well go on to the target now that you had this much invested. This was the meteorologist equivalent of "work your way down through the Alps".

Usually we could break clear over the field in the race track pattern, form up and start across the Adriatic in the clear and then hit the soup over Yugoslavia.

There would be your seven ship box heading into a solid black cloud mass, accompanied by the other twenty-one ships from your group, accompanied by twenty-eight ships from each of the other three bomb groups of the 47th Wing, accompanied by 28 ships from the other seventeen groups from the 15th Air Force.

In other words, there were five hundred plus airplanes milling around in the muck.

In my wildest dreams, I never imagined anything like high altitude instrument formation flying. Fearless Red said we were going to get good and by god he was right.

You knew that once you went into the soup that there was nothing you could do but continue. If you tried to pull out, or up, or down, you would risk hitting a plane from another group which you couldn't see but you knew was there somewhere.

It was like two fencers slashing away at one another with sabres in a dark room.

As soon as you entered the clouds, you would lose sight of the plane you were flying on; you would then start edging back in toward your leader inch by inch. Suddenly, you'd see him and you would be right on top of him -- you'd then jerk the plane out and away to prevent a collision; you would thus lose sight of him and of necessity start inching back till you gained sight -- jerked away, etc.

I kept this up for three to four hours many times. Usually you'd break out on top at about 20,000 to 22,000 feet where you'd break into the clear. So at least you didn't have to fly the bomb run under these conditions.

This is the most nerve racking type of flying I've ever done -- believe me, you sweat blood doing it. Oddly enough, while you thought you were going to hit someone any minute, you never did. I never heard of a single mid-air collision from this kind of flying although conditions similar to this existed on about half the missions I flew.

18.

A target at Vienna, Austria is hit by the 450th Bomb Group Liberators. (Vincent Fagan collection)

I didn't like camera men.

There must have been some clean-cut, bright-eyed, All-American types -- but I never met any.

Occasionally, a camera man would be assigned to our crew. It was his function to install a large camera over the camera hatch in the waist of the plane. He would switch on the camera at the beginning of the bomb run which would then obtain pictures of the bomb run and the position of the bomb strikes on the target.

For some reason or other, we were never informed that a camera man had been assigned to our crew. In addition, the camera man would never come up to the pilot and make his presence known. You'd find out about him from talk on the inter-phone or in some other round-about manner.

I never could understand why these mostly flaky characters could not come up, introduce themselves, shake hands, and make themselves known, but they never did.

We were off and running to Vienna one day and were at about 16,000 feet over Yugoslavia. Over the interphone comes my first contact from the typical invisible camera man: "Camera man to pilot, over."

"Go ahead, camera man," I replied.

"Sir, I am out of oxygen," he said.

I looked at my oxygen, about 250 pounds. How in the hell can he be out of oxygen. He was on a separate system, one of six throughout the plane.

"Camera man, plug into a walk-around bottle temporarily till I figure out what to do," I said to him on the interphone.

"Ball turret to pilot -- I'm also out of oxygen," this from Van Lowell in the ball turret.

This figured; the ball turret and waist camera position were on the same system.

"Yeah Van, come on up out of the ball, retract the ball and plug into a walk-around bottle till I figure out what we're going to do," I said.

I sat there trying to figure out what the hell was going on -- how could these two guys use up 1/6 of our total oxygen supply when I hadn't used 1/3 of my system. It just didn't make sense. I knew in a minute what it was all about.

"Camera man to pilot, over," came over the interphone.

"Go ahead, camera man," I said.

"Sir, are we going to turn around and go back?" he asked.

I knew at once he had had a massive attack of the heebie-jeebies and was in no mood to go to Vienna. He had deliberately turned on the emergency selector valve and bled the system, thinking I'd turn back without oxygen.

"Camera man," I said, "did you turn on the emergency selector valve?" I shouted at him on the interphone.

"Yes Sir," he replied, "I wasn't getting enough oxygen so I wanted to blow some air in my face." This bleeds the entire system in two minutes.

"Van," I called.

"Yes Lieutenant," from Van Lowell.

"Bring that son-of-a-bitch up to the flight deck and plug him into my system. If he touches the oxygen selector valve, throw him overboard," I said.

"Camera man," I continued.

"Yes, Sir," from the now nervous camera man.

"Camera man, you're going to come up here and use my oxygen since you have thrown all yours away. If you attempt to screw up my system, you are going to walk home. Do you understand me?" I said.

"Yes, Sir" from the camera man.

I forgot about him and went on the mission; when we landed, he took off. I never even bothered to find out his name. I knew he'd never be back.

He was scared and didn't want to go on the mission and thought that by bleeding his oxygen system he'd provided me with an excuse to turn around and go back. Everyone could use an excuse to walk away from Vienna.

I'm glad Van hadn't thrown him overboard and I hadn't meant it literally, though technically he was guilty of sabotage and Fearless Red would have chopped him up in little tiny pieces in his meat grinder. I never saw the son-of-a-bitch again -- but then I never ever saw him in the first place.

19.

A 15th Air Force Liberator of the 376th Bomb Group beneath others in its formation on a mission to Toulon, France, June 8, 1944.

Usually after you had 25 or so missions, new pilots arriving with a crew from the States would be assigned to fly with you on one or two missions till they got the feel of things, then they were turned loose to solo with their own crew. I flew with a half dozen new pilots in this fashion. It was astonishing the difference in their level of skill even though they all had been through the same training program.

A new pilot by the name of Haggerty had been assigned to me and I had been warned by a couple of my friends who had flown with him that he wasn't real bright.

We were going to Munich and we were flying #4 in the box -- below and behind the leader, a very easy position to fly. He flew part of the time and seemed to do all right.

As we started down the bomb run, we simultaneously got a runaway prop on one engine and a runaway supercharger on another engine. I turned the flying over to Haggerty and started trying to correct the prop and supercharger malfunction. I had my head down inside the cockpit for a while when I glanced over at my illustrious co-pilot.

His head was stretched straight back and he was looking up through the plexiglass roof of the cockpit. It hit me like ten tons of bricks, he had completely underrun the lead ship! With bombs ready to go away any second, the bomb bay doors open and the target coming up, he had blithely run under the open bomb bay of the lead ship. And having thus won the all time high altitude, colossal stupidity award he was about to try dropping back under the lead ship again by chopping the power!

For even as I took in this situation, he cut the throttles and was about to run underneath again in the opposite direction to get back in correct position. Just as he did this, I grabbed the wheel and slammed on full throttle.

We pulled out in front again and wound up leading the bomb run from below the lead ship.

An airplane being bombed like this happened several times for various reasons.

While the bombs would not explode when they hit the plane below, they usually broke up the wing and/or the wing tanks causing an explosion.

After bombs went away, we rallied right with the group and managed to get back into position.

No one called me and asked the reason for our insane maneuvers. This was considered bad form. It was always thought that you had some mechanical problems which caused such gyrations rather than lack of flying skill.

The most surprising thing about this deal was that Haggerty came through it completely unperturbed. It didn't bother him a bit; he didn't even ask why I took over the plane after he had underrun the lead ship the first time.

Shortly after this, Haggerty was sent out with his own crew and blew up over Vienna, my nose gunner with him, unfortunately.

20.

It seemed that every time I went up at night, I had a fire on a B-24. This tradition was started early in the game at Boise where I had five fires in night flying.

This, plus the fact that interior lighting on a B-24 was almost non-existent, also greatly prejudiced me against night operations.

Someone dreamed up a deal called "Night Intruder Missions". Each squadron was to send one crew equipped with bombing radar to places like Klagenfurt, Innsbruck, and Munich to bomb. The object was not destruction but intimidation. Keep the Germans awake all night.

Corporal Cicero, "El Supremo", stopped me one day and asked if I would like to sign up for night intruder missions. He extolled all the virtues -- no formation flying, weather no hazard since you could fly instruments, and you could finish your missions in a hurry since in theory you could fly every day.

I told him that when he had asked all the other pilots in the squadron to go, and when they had court-martialed all of them and put them in Leavenworth for refusing to go, to come back and I'd give him an answer.

I knew that he had sent five individual crews up north to the Klagenfurt area and that once off the ground we had never heard anything from them again.

What I didn't know was that the Germans had night fighters equipped with radar to seek out and fire on such B-24's while our gunners sat in the turrets straining their eyes in the dark with no radar to sight and fire back.

I found this out after the war --- so much for night intruder missions.

21.

Flak seeks out B-24s of the Italy-based 449th Bomb Group on a raid over Europe.

The great destroyer in our life was flak.

German 88 millimeter cannon would fire shells at us repeatedly at the rate of six every ten seconds.

As the war wound down for Germany the concentration of flak guns increased. When Ploesti fell, the guns were pulled back up north. No flak guns were ever left behind as Germany lost territory.

At one stage of the game, there were 600 88 millimeter

flak guns at Vienna. These guns were radar controlled with an accuracy and frequency that was extremely discouraging.

Flak was strange stuff. Frequently you would hear five or six explosions beneath your plane and the plane would jump five or ten feet from the explosion yet there would be no marks on the plane.

Another time you would hear nothing, yet you'd have fifty holes in the plane.

Again, you would hear it splatter all over the plane -- it would sound as if someone had thrown a handful of gravel on a tin roof. Yet again, you could rarely find a hole in the plane from this.

Most of us acquired souvenir pieces which were usually a cube about an inch square but of course very irregular.

We were told that there were quite a few duds due to the disgruntled slave laborers working on them.

Our squadron commander, Vance Durbin, was killed on a bomb run by a piece of flak about a foot in diameter and about an inch thick. It completely took his chest out, yet his co-pilot was uninjured.

A great invention that came along was called "window" or "chaff". These were small packets of tin foil similar to that used on Christmas trees though a little stiffer. When thrown over board on the bomb run, it showed up as a B-24 on the German radar and diluted the flak by that amount.

The gunners were instructed to throw out three packets every 20 seconds. No German or American fighters entered the flak area so the gunners didn't have too much to do on the bomb run.

Most of them reasoned that if three packets every 20 seconds was good, then six packets in 10 seconds was better, etc. Pretty soon you could hardly get into the rear end of a B-24 from all the chaff stored there and huge areas of Germany were covered with Christmas tree foil.

I didn't know whether it did any good but it kept the gunners busy and was a comforting shield.

The worst flak area that the 15th Air Force hit was Vienna. You could fly 125 miles in a straight line and be under constant, intense 88 mm fire. A very traumatic experience.

22.

The great invention that kept long range, day time, heavy bombardment alive, was the long range fighter escort.

In the 15th Air Force, these were mostly P-51s with a few P-38s on occasion. These were certainly a welcome sight on a mission. The Germans had set up Ju-88s to sit out of .50 caliber machine gun range and lob rockets into the formations. The fighter escorts put a stop to this crap.

In addition, after flying escort, a P-51 could go down on the deck and strafe and still have enough gas to get home.

Germany had 5,000 Me-109's at the end of the war -- they lacked gas to operate them and gas to train people to fly them. They were sending pilots into combat in an Me-109 with 75 hours flying time.

At the end of 1944, two very disquieting airplanes were showing up in the sky around Munich -- the Me-163 rocket-powered fighter and the Me-262 jet fighter -- 200 m.p.h. faster than our fighters.

Usually we saw them about 12,000 feet above us, emitting short puffs of vapor trails. We heard they didn't attack because the armament hadn't been upgraded to operate at their speed. A few whiffs of these characters and it seemed to make sense to get your missions over with and get the hell home.

Most P-51's didn't come in too close to the bomber formations. Not that they looked all that much like an Me-109 but they did have a similar configuration and most turret gunners would simply fire at anything and ask questions later. After getting whacked by heavy bomber squadrons a few times, most American fighter pilots learned to stay well out of range. but it still stuck in their craw that Americans would shoot at them and they didn't like it.

One day we ran very low on gas on the way back from Vienna and put in at a fighter strip up north near Foggia.

We went over to the Red Cross doughnut stand to get some coffee. Nearby stood several P-51 pilots. Our nose gunner and eminent shit distributor went over to them and pointed to Spaak, our tail gunner and said, proudly and falsely, "See that tail gunner of ours -- name's Spaak. He's got three P-51's to his credit."

We got the matter straightened out finally.

23.

A 451st Bomb Group Lib belly-lands at its base at Castellucio, Italy following a Ploesti mission.

Everything improved when the bombs went away -- the plane was 5,000 or 6,000 pounds lighter, we were leaving the flak instead of going into it and we could take evasive action -- usually a diving turn towards the shortest escape route from the flak area.

It was much easier flying formation going downhill and I frequently let Bob Felker and Rod do the flying while I sat on the flight deck with Driggs and had something to eat. Usually we'd open a can of tomato juice deliciously flecked with ice crystals from the cold and break out some ten-in-one rations.

It always griped me that not only did the Army not give you any food to take on an eight hour mission but they charged you 33 cents for the so-called lunch they served back at the base that you weren't there to eat.

When I say that it wasn't the money but the principle of the thing, it becomes understandable when I say that in nine months overseas I spent less than $100.

Usually the trip back was pleasant if there were no mechanical problems, no fighters, and the only hazardous part was the actual landing itself. Here again the Army had taught us a very impractical landing approach. It was great for airlines but terrible for combat.

We would peel off in seven ship boxes and swing around in a large circle and land flying the final approach at 500 feet and 130 m.p.h. and pull it onto the runway with power from five or ten miles out.

It seemed to me that if the critical three engine speed was 145 m.p.h., then it was silly to get below it, so I flew the final approach at 150 m.p.h. and stayed at that speed, altitude 1,000 feet, until I could cut the throttles and glide onto the runway. Most of the other pilots I knew used this system.

A few didn't. One day one of the drag-it-in boys came across the fence at 130 m.p.h. -- started to flare out over the end of the runway at about 50 feet altitude -- the ship stalled and splattered all over the end of the runway.

The ship broke up with wings, engines and fuselage going in various directions.

Upon later investigation, it was discovered that the airspeed indicator was off 20 m.p.h., reading that much too high. Once again reinforcing my feeling that the more air speed you had in a B-24, the better off you were. And that advice you got from on high to fool around at low altitude at a low airspeed should be ignored. Suggestions for low turns and low airspeed should absolutely be ignored.

Unfortunately, most landings were rather hectic -- ships with engines out or wounded on board or low on fuel were all competing for the right to land first. The tower would usually try to sort them out and ask one or two of them to pull up and go around in the interest of safety.

No matter how close two or three ships were to one another on the final approach and no matter how much screaming was going on over the radio, I never saw anyone ever pull up and go around -- can't say I blame them. I wouldn't have done it either, though I never got involved in this situation.

Occasionally it became necessary to bring a plane over the field and, instead of landing it, jump the crew.

Usually they'd parachute over the field from about 1,000 feet and for some reason or other that never was determined, this operation usually killed at least one crew member. In addition, they always seemed to break at least one guy's leg.

Joe Eagan ended his tour with a very flamboyant landing.

He had two engines out and decided to land on a fighter base up north of Foggia. As he set up for his final approach, the fighter tower started yelling at him over the radio that the strip was too short for a B-24 landing and started firing red flares at him. Since the alternative was to crash land in the open country, Eagan ignored all this and came on in.

As promised, the steel runway was a little short and Eagan wound up slamming into a revetment and smashing up the nose and severing the nose wheel.

No one was hurt, so Joe climbed out to survey the damage.

A colonel pulled up in a Jeep and started raising hell with Joe for landing there when the tower warned him off. Joe replied that he had just finished his 50th mission and couldn't care what the Colonel thought.

A curious footnote to the affair is that the Bomb Group sent a ground crew up there to repair the plane. They worked on it for three months and finally got it fixed.

The Group sent a pilot up there, he took off, flew it back to Frantic and crashed it on landing, completely demolishing it this time.

24.

A 15th Air Force 98th Bomb Group B-24.

More B-24s were built in World War II than any other airplane -- approximately 18,000. I have often wondered why.

Not that the plane looked all that bad -- the single tail model built for the Navy, "The Privateer", looked pretty sharp.

It had Pratt and Whitney engines and in this respect it was superior to the B-17 with its Wright engines.

No matter how long you flew it, it always seemed as if it

was about to turn around and bite you.

Mostly it had very little safety margin. The original Davis airfoil concept was great if you gave the pilot the weight saved with the smaller, more efficient laminar flow wing as a safety factor.

But not only did the pilot not get this advantage, as more turrets, gasoline, armor plate, etc. were added, but he received the disadvantage that relatively high speeds had to be maintained to gain any efficiency and in the event of a lost engine or two, you could not maintain altitude by slowing up the plane but only by pouring on more coal to the subsequent risk of further damage to engines that were still functioning.

I never flew a B-17 and can't argue its merits from personal experience. There were many instances of a B-17 losing two engines over a target and coming all the way home, 700 or 800 miles.

I never heard of this happening in a B-24. Every instance of a two engine landing with a B-24 that I had heard of, it turned out that one engine was lost over the target and the other one pretty far down the line on the way back.

The B-17/B-24 argument will never be settled but I think if they had let the pilots pick which one they wanted to fly, there sure as hell would have been a lot less than 18,000 B-24's produced.

25.

Using crew parachutes to slow its landing roll, a 304th Bomb Wing Liberator returns to its Italy base.

I never ever wanted to fly a B-24 in the first place.

When we were finishing the aviation cadet program at Altus, Oklahoma, we were told to start giving some thought as to what plane we wanted to fly after we graduated. The implication was that we could pretty much count on being assigned to whatever plane we selected.

My own feeling was that I'd like to wind up in a P-38

twin engine fighter, or an A-20 or B-25 light twin engine bomber. I simply didn't consider a four engine bomber.

I had gone all the way through cadets with six other fellows who had become very firm friends, Feld, Faber, Freeman, Finch, French and Froelich. They came to me and said that for various reasons they had decided to put in for B-24's and asked me to do the same so that we could all stay together. I thought this was a lousy idea but decided to go along with the program when I couldn't talk them out of it.

Came the day just before graduation to turn in our preference to the Air Force in writing. I thought what the hell, if I'm going to put down B-24 for first choice, I might as well back it up with four engine choices, which I did by selecting B-17 second choice, and C-54 third choice.

I checked with my friends to see if they had gone the four engine B-24 route. With the exception of Feld, they had all weaseled out at the last minute and picked out some small twin engine job as their first choice and I was going to be the great B-24 guinea pig of the group. When we graduated, not only had this group gone on without me but I was stuck with the B-24.

We graduated and I received my orders to go to B-24 1st Pilot training at Tarrant Field, Ft. Worth, Texas.

I was despondent but my despondency eased when I found out a few days later that all the options of various types of planes were just so much window dressing. There were only two slots for our class -- B-24 1st pilots and B-24 co-pilots.

Anyone who asked for B-24's was assigned B-24 1st pilot school, the rest of the class were made B-24 co-pilots.

Including my buddies.

26.

The author at Manduria, Italy with his Neo-Sicilian Moderne house.

We decided to build the house in Neo-Sicilian Moderne.

That is to say, Dan and I scratched a line on the ground with a stick to mark off an area 20 feet x 20 feet, with a door, windows, fireplace, and walk-in closet marked out.

This ended the planning phase with our two stone masons, Giuseppe and Julio. We had a mission the next day so they'd be on their own starting out. We told them to start laying the caliche blocks we had bought until they used them all up or we got back.

Giuseppe was a happy, effervescent type and Julio, a brooding, sullen, anti-American; "un molto Facisti".

We couldn't speak Italian and they couldn't speak English so it was sort of a phrase book romance, so to speak. Giuseppe and Julio were each to receive $1.25 per day since they were skilled workmen; their helper was to receive 75 cents per day since he was merely an unskilled laborer.

Economics was not the problem -- there were thornier issues.

First you had to obtain approval from the squadron to build on a specific piece of land. Even though you paid all the costs of the house, the Army technically owned it and could kick you out any time they wanted. This was theory. Actually, the Squadron welcomed your house building adventure since it took some pressure off the rickety barracks.

When Dan Driggs and I decided to build the house, we approached Major Bascom, Squadron Administrative Officer, for his blessing; he insisted that we take in a third person in exchange for which the Squadron would furnish a truck for material hauling. We designated Bob Crowe, our navigator, as our third owner and resident and he lived in the house with us until he had his feet amputated for frostbite and returned to the States. He sold his interest in the house to Joe Eagan, a pilot friend of ours who then moved in.

The big problem was acquisition of material. Caliche

blocks were cut out of a local quarry by hand. They were about the size of a modern concrete block about 8" x 8" x 16" and cost eight cents each. Caliche was a soft, sandstone easily cut and shaped.

Every waking moment for two months was dedicated to getting our hands on a truck and hauling caliche blocks back to the home site from the quarry.

One day we went to the quarry, bought a load of blocks, had them stacked on the truck and as we were driving away, we glanced back and one of the Italians who sold them to us, was sitting on the truck throwing the blocks off on the road. We stopped. Driggs went back and I thought he would kill the son-of-a-bitch. Driggs was a real gentleman except in situations like this.

We got the walls up. Got the walls plastered, got the floor concreted -- we even found a 24 foot, 6 x 6 ridge pole -- a monumental achievement as there is almost no lumber in southern Italy. All that remained was the corrugated sheet steel for the roof.

We were instructed by Major Bascom to go down and see Corporal Jackson, "the Squadron Thief", and tell him that Bascom said we were to get the steel we needed.

We found Jackson, delivered Bascom's message and asked for the steel. After much moaning and groaning by Jackson, we went out in back of his tent where a huge lumber yard existed and Jackson reluctantly gave us our steel. This seemed a peculiar arrangement.

I later found out that the British controlled most of the supplies coming into Italy and that on a legitimate basis, the Bomb Group could not get their hands on any building material or hardly any other supplies except airplanes and gasoline. Through some fluke of circumstance, Jackson had become acquainted with some of the British who ran the docks at Taranto.

The squadron agreed to furnish Jackson with a truck and gasoline in exchange for half the building material he stole from the British, he kept the other half and sold it on the black market.

I don't know what he was supposed to be doing in the Army, but this was a full-time job with him -- stealing American lend-lease building material for himself and the Squadron from the British off the docks at Taranto.

We got the roof on, installed the electricity, and moved in our G.I. cots with their straw mattresses and the custom-built chairs and couch we had ordered in Bari when they were delivered. We furnished the G.I. blankets and mattress covers that were dyed and used to upholster the furniture. Half the Italians in Italy were clothed in ex-G.I. blankets and mattress covers.

The house was really terrific -- beautiful. We had rugs on the floor -- felt airplane insulation -- and I built a desk out of plywood bomb bay luggage carriers.

We burned pressed paper bomb rings in the fireplace every night and acquired Gregorio -- a fifteen year old major-domo who took care of the place.

The complete cost of the house including all the furniture and rugs, was $135.

27.

MISSION LOG

(Missions are consecutive --- double numbers indicate double mission credit).

#1 BUDAPEST - July 27, 1944
Covered previously in the text.

#2 PLOESTI - July 31, 1944
Bombed Targoviste, part of the Ploesti complex. Flew co-pilot for Lt. Vance and crew. Were hit by a few bits of flak over the coast of Yugoslavia. Engines kept overheating on way to the target. Very little flak on bomb run and almost none over target.

#3 & #4 VIENNA - September 10, 1944
Had trouble getting off. Flew co-pilot for Lt. Welker and finally had to take a spare when #3 engine wouldn't start in first plane. Got off half hour late. Caught formation and got in position as group started on course. We flew #2 position so I had to fly cross cockpit and consequently I didn't do much flying.

Hit with flak on bomb run; as I looked out to my right the wing blew off a nearby 24 which started spinning; no one got out.

The flak was extremely heavy and very accurate. My

108

feet were very cold. My crew was flown by Lt. Lang and Tar, our waist gunner, bailed out on the bomb run thinking the plane was on fire. Later heard he was killed in the air by flak.

#5 LARISSA, GREECE - September 15, 1944
Very easy mission -- almost no flak and no fighters. We were supposed to bomb railroad marshalling yards to prevent the Germans from escaping back into the Balkans from Crete.

Flew over Albania and Northern Greece which must be some of the roughest terrain in the world.

#6 BUDAPEST - September 18, 1944
Target was one of the bridges over the Danube between Buda and Pest. Got caught in a lot of prop wash during assembly; had a runaway supercharger on the way to the target.

We made the bomb run at 25,500 -- the flak wasn't too accurate but the group behind us caught hell. For the first time I saw the target prior to the bomb run.

#7 & #8 MALACKY, CZECHOSLOVAKIA - September 20, 1944
We flew #5 and had a difficult time trying to get into formation because of cloud coverage over the field. Carried fragmentation bombs to bomb airplanes on the airfield which was the target.

A lot of flak came up until the first groups dropped their frag bombs and then it stopped. We found this to be nearly always the case when we dropped frag bombs; whether it killed the flak gunners or they ran for the brush, I don't know.

#9 LARISSA, GREECE - September 22, 1944
Went back after the same marshalling yard that was weathered in on Mission #5.

Very difficult assembly because of bad weather.

On the bomb run, we caught several close bursts, yet there were no holes in the ship.

#10 & #11 VIENNA - October 7, 1944
Target: Winterhaven Oil Storage Depot on an island in the Danube. We lost the Squadron Commander, Squadron Navigator and Squadron Bombardier when the lead ship went down over the target. Our group lost six airplanes today.

My oxygen hose pulled out on the bomb run and I passed out from lack of oxygen. Bob Felker, co-pilot, took over and flew the plane while Rod came down from the upper deck turret and plugged me back into the oxygen. We staggered around in the formation until we got everything under control -- we were lucky not to hit one of the other planes.

A very rough mission.

#12 VIENNA - October 11, 1944
Mission fouled up by weather. Bombed from solid overcast at 26,000 feet.

#13 BOLOGNA - October 12, 1944
A long drawn out mission from one side of Italy to the other parallel to the front lines. Under continuous flak attack most of the time.

#14 BANHIDA, HUNGARY - October 13, 1944
A real screwed-up mission -- went over the target twice. A new low in leadership. Missed fighter escort and were dogged by German fighters all the way. The group behind us got jumped and got the hell shot out of them.

#15 & #16 STEYR, AUSTRIA - October 17, 1944
Lead ship got lost and we wandered all over Germany and Austria before making bomb run. Our fighter escort finally got disgusted and left us.

#17 BRENNER PASS - October 23, 1944
Ploughed through a lot of weather but didn't bomb because of low undercast. Carried booby trap time fuses and dropped them in Adriatic on way home.

#18 PODGORICA, YUGOSLAVIA - October 31, 1944
Milk run 150 miles across the Adriatic. Went over and

back twice but didn't drop bombs because of weather.

#19 & #20 MUNICH - November 4, 1944

Target: West marshalling yard. A lot of flak as always at Munich but not nearly as accurate as Vienna.

#21 & #22 VIENNA - November 5, 1944

Target: Florisdorf oil refinery. A very long bomb run and a lot of flak.

#23 & #24 VIENNA - November 6, 1944

Very heavy flak with several bursts so close they made us blink.

#25 METROVICA, YUGOSLAVIA - November 8, 1944

Milk run -- didn't drop bombs because of low undercast.

#26 SJENICA, YUGOSLAVIA - November 16, 1944

Couldn't bomb. Radar ship turned back and target cloud covered.

#27 & #28 VIENNA - November 17, 1944

Didn't get to Vienna. Lost #3 engine short of the target and bombed Waldheim by myself while group continued on to target.

#29 AVIANO, ITALY - November 18, 1944

Dropped frag bombs and got good hits on target.

#30 & #31 VIENNA - November 19, 1944
Target: Schwechat Oil refinery. Radar bomb run was no good so we wound up bombing marshalling yard at Gyer, Austria.

#32 DOBOJ, YUGOSLAVIA - November 21, 1944
Shortest mission flown -- lasted about four hours. Bad weather so no bombs dropped on bridge for which we were briefed.

#33 SJENICA, YUGOSLAVIA November 23, 1944
Thanksgiving Day -- milk run and turkey when we got back to Frantic.

#34 & #35 VIENNA - December 8, 1944
Lost #2 engine on way home but got it running again.

#36 & #37 INNSBRUCK - December 16, 1944
First mission since back from rest camp. Bombed main marshalling yard.

#38 & #39 VIENNA - December 18, 1944
Target: Florisdorf oil refinery. Not much flak but fighters hit one group hard.

#40 SALZBURG, AUSTRIA - December 20, 1944
Easy mission -- a lot of weather. Flew over Hitler's retreat at Berchtesgaden.

#41 INNSBRUCK - December 25, 1944

Down,

Down,

Goddammit, down.

28.

THE END OF THE END

We staggered away from Innsbruck at 19,000 feet, heading west and still losing 5,000 feet per minute, two engines out, neither props feathered.

Lowell, the radio operator, called from the waist and suggested we make a run for Yugo. I told him it was out of the question -- we couldn't clear the Alps. He then asked if it was okay to start throwing things overboard. I told him to dump anything they could, including the ball turret. They started chopping things up with axes, but they never did get rid of the ball turret.

Partly as a result of everything they threw overboard, our situation began to improve. They threw out all the machine gun ammunition, the .50 caliber machine guns from the waist windows, emergency oxygen bottles, all the side arms and personal medical kits, flak suits, etc.

They opened the camera hatch, which is about four feet square, and were ready to use it to bail out. It's in the floor and provides an excellent exit from which to parachute from the rear of a B-24.

I called the navigator and asked him to give me a heading to Switzerland. "No dice," he replied, "I don't have any maps for that area and my compass is out."

I told him to come up on the flight deck and tear open one of the escape kits and use that map.

I knew that Switzerland was due west of Innsbruck about 90 miles -- 30 minutes or so at this air speed. I didn't think we could make it that far or stay in the air that long but we might as well be heading someplace and put some distance between ourselves and the unhappy citizens of Innsbruck. I did not want to jump at Innsbruck if they were in a hanging mood as Intelligence had said.

We were about ten miles north of the Alps and I planned on staying there at least a few miles north of them. I had no desire to parachute into fifty feet of snow to be rescued next spring by the local natives. The terrain was so forbidding that by mutual unspoken agreement, neither American bombers nor German fighter planes fired at each other over the Alps.

I increased the power on #3 and #4; shoved everything forward to full high-props, throttles, turbos and mixture. I was indicating one hundred sixty miles per hour. I decided to see what I could do about improving our altitude loss.

I dropped ten degrees of flaps, sucked back on the wheel and we slowed down to one hundred forty-five miles per hour, which was supposed to be the critical three engine speed or that speed below which you could not maintain direction control.

We were still in a forty-five degree bank attitude but our altitude loss dropped from five thousand feet per minute to twenty-five hundred feet per minute.

I decided to slow it down again and dropped the air speed to one hundred forty; to one hundred thirty and finally to one hundred twenty-five miles per hour. I didn't have enough courage to slow it down any more and would never have believed this could be done with two engines out.

At that, the controls were pretty sloppy at 125 miles per hour and we were pretty close to stalling speed.

We were now at thirteen thousand feet when up ahead and to our right I could see a tremendous lake --- Lake Constance.

I knew the boundary of Switzerland and Germany ran the length of Lake Constance. There was a slot in front of us between the Alps and the lake. All we had to do was run through that slot and we'd be in Switzerland.

In five minutes, Hallins, the navigator, came up with an

escape map he'd found, pointing out various check points proving we were indeed approaching the Swiss border.

I began to get dreams of overflying Switzerland and on to France past the front lines at the Rhine. Far up ahead loomed a large and threatening undercast and that dream dissolved. I had no interest in going into a cloud layer with no gyro instruments and two engines out.

I knew there was an airport at Zurich, so we set out to find it. Switzerland is a small country and Zurich a big city, but we never did find it.

By now, we were down to about 8,500 feet. I told the crew that if we didn't find Zurich by the time we hit 5,000 feet, we'd jump. Meanwhile, we'd keep looking. I thought sure we'd find it, but we never did.

March jerked his thumb for a quick turn to the right and all hell broke loose again.

We were in a terrific flak attack. I had never seen small caliber flak before -- probably 20 mm or 48 mm; but it was incredible the amount that came up. We were over Wurenlingen, Switzerland where the Aare River joins the Rhine, on the German-Swiss border. The Germans were clobbering us from their side of the river while the Swiss were giving us hell from their side.

The Swiss were entirely within their rights banging away at us; I met the Captain of the Wurenlingen flak batteries some days later, he took credit for shooting us down rather than the Germans.

In addition, our bomb bay doors were open, which wasn't the friendliest sight; if we really were intending to surrender we should have been firing flares -- but I couldn't risk this with all the gas leaks.

While the Swiss were officially neutral, like most Americans I always thought that they were secretly on our side. I found out that they were openly and avowedly on their own side -- and quite capable of defending their position from a military standpoint.

I tried a few turns to see if I could shake the flak but I couldn't get out of it. I counted five good hits that pounded into the plane, and I decided that we had all we could take. One good direct hit and we'd explode with all the gas leaks.

I hit the gear handle to indicate surrender. No go. The gear would not go down. We weren't going to land at Zurich anyway, with no wheels.

Just then, the number two engine fell off the wing, having lost too much oil, it had vibrated itself to pieces. I called the crew and told them to bail out.

The engineer, co-pilot, and navigator went out in that order from the flight deck, the rest from the waist.

My seat would not slide back so I climbed over the throttle quadrant, pulled the number four throttle off so the plane would stay on course, moved back to the bomb bay where Hallins, the navigator, was standing, getting ready to jump. He went out and then it was my turn.

It was like standing on a ten foot diving board -- the longer you stood there, the longer you looked, the harder it is to jump. I thought briefly of going back and flying the damned thing.

The only thing that made any sense now was to get out.

I put my hand in my parachute "D" ring and spun out through the bomb bay. I hit the slip stream and was spinning rapidly. I stiffened my body into a full lay out to slow down the spinning.

I yanked the "D" ring and the chute opened with a terrific wallop. The back of the harness knocked my head down to my chest and the front metal turnbuckle smashed into my mouth -- splitting my lips and bloodying my nose and mouth badly.

I counted six chutes open below me and then heard and saw the plane far below, down on the deck -- headed straight towards the town of Wurenlingen.

The plane slammed into an open area on the edge of town and exploded violently.

Inexplicably, the bodies of Moe Hallins, the navigator, and Harry Cool, the waist gunner, were later found in the wreckage of the plane, while co-pilot Ned March drowned in the Aare River.

The rest of us slowly drifted to the ground where we hit Switzerland about a mile inside the Swiss border.

The only pleasant memory that I have of this entire mission is the parachute descent after "Maiden America" hit the ground.

I hung there suspended by the shrouds with no sensation of falling or any kind of motion. Absolute peace, absolute quiet.

For the first time in hours there was no noise or vibration beating in on me, no demands being made on me and no disaster impending.

Christmas was gone -- the mission was over.

AFTERWARD

Vincent Fagan's crew as internees at Adelboden, Switzerland. Author is center, standing. (Vincent Fagan collection)

I slammed into the vertical bank of the Aare River while my chute caught on a tree and stopped me just short of the water.

A dozen or so Swiss soldiers, accompanied by a large contingent of local citizenry for whom we had put on quite a show, picked me up. They took me to a border patrol station where they informed me that March had drowned in the Aare River and that Cool and Hallins had crashed with the plane.

I could buy the story that March had drowned because I had just missed the river myself, but I could not understand how Hallins and Cool could be in the wreckage of the plane. Both of them had plenty of time to get out and I had seen Hallins jump out the bomb bay right in front of me.

This mystery was never solved. Cool was the last man out of the waist and may have been disabled by flak before he jumped, but how Hallins wound up inside the wreckage has never been explained. He should have hit the ground close to me, instead he was inside the plane wreckage a half mile away.

The Swiss at first refused to let me go look at the wreckage. I wanted to see Cool and Hallins bodies to make sure that they had been identified properly. I kept agitating to go to the crash site and finally the Swiss took me over there about two hours after we had jumped.

The plane hit in a small park on the edge of town; there was a burnt area about 150 feet in diameter which was still smoking. There were three large holes in the ground where the engines hit --- there was not a piece of the plane left any bigger than a silver dollar except an aluminum panel with the name of the plane -- "Maiden America".

I checked Cool and Hallins dog tags and then the Swiss took me back to the border station.

We buried Moe, Ned and Harry at the American Military Cemetery in Munsingen, Switzerland, three days later and their bodies were brought back to the States after the war.

The rest of us were interned in a dead end canyon at Adelboden till the end of February, 1945 when we were exchanged for German internees - mostly infantry who had been trapped in Switzerland as a result of the invasion of Southern France.

Nevada Palace Hotel, Adelboden, Switzerland, where the author's crew was interned. (Vincent Fagan collection)

I spent the balance of the war in the Air Transport Command flying C-47's (DC-3's) hospital ships coast to coast in the United States.

A 450th Bomb Group B-24H with "Cottontail" markings wings its way over snowy terrain.

EPILOGUE

Why do they do it? Why do men go off to war and fight -- someone has answered because women are watching.

Perhaps.

I think it would be closer to the mark to say because men are watching.

Then there's making the world safe for democracy, mom and apple pie, and the right to boo the Dodgers.

In my case it was none of these unless these reasons were subconscious.

I had been interested in aviation and combat flying since 'way back in the early thirties with movies like

"Wings" and "Dawn Patrol" plus a good deal of reading on the subject.

At the start of the war I had read about Richard Hillary in the Battle of Britain, George Beurling at Malta, Colin Kelly and the battleship *Haruna*, and George Gay of Torpedo Squadron Eight at the battle of Midway.

I held these men in high esteem and marvelled that they could perform so well in such appalling circumstances. However, the idea of being a hot shot pilot in combat or personally carrying the war to the enemy was a very postponable idea as far as I was concerned.

After I graduated from cadets and was in B-24 training, I used to occasionally hear some guy say he couldn't wait to get to combat. This puzzled me because I couldn't believe it was a genuine sentiment -- and, in the main, the way I saw pilots like this perform later in combat, it wasn't a true expression of their desires. I had no illusions about combat and therefore wasn't disappointed when I saw what it was like.

The original grind down of numbers started for me at 20 years old on July 21, 1942, when I went down to the Federal Building in St. Louis to take the written and physical exams for Pilot Training in the Army Air Corps.

One hundred and thirty-five of us showed up that morning; at the end of the day 13 were sworn in as cadets -- the balance eliminated.

A few more were eliminated during classification and pre-flight the following February at San Antonio.

In Primary Flight Training in Muskogee, Oklahoma,

48% of the class of 150 were washed out; in Basic Flight Training at Coffeyville, Kansas, 30% of the class of 150 were washed out. Only one guy washed out in Advanced at Altus, Oklahoma.

Of the original 135 that showed up at the Federal Building, perhaps two or three ever graduated from pilot training.

To survive in a program like this you had to fight like hell and work like hell or the Air Corps would simply give you the large good-bye.

By the time I hit the 450th bomb group something like $400,000 had been expended on my training including B-24 time.

When I got to Italy and edged toward the precipice, a small voice said, "Why me?" -- another voice answered, "Who else?"

As far as I was concerned, you didn't have to have a great hankering for combat; you had accepted the training -- fought for it as a matter of fact -- now it was your turn to perform, by flying the stipulated number of missions.

It is not possible, in my opinion, to teach someone how to fly combat.

In the final analysis you must teach yourself.

You can be taught certain flying maneuvers and techniques but the primary thing involved is an act of your own will.

You must first make an absolute, massive determination that come hell or high water you are going to fly the mission assigned to you -- you are going to go where they tell you to go, bomb what they tell you to bomb and then try to get yourself and your crew back in one piece.

Unless you do this you become an "abort expert" -- an early return artist.

But when you make a commitment to go no matter what, your mind starts concentrating on flying improvement, efficiency and survival rather than looking for subtle reasons to stay on the ground or turn around and go back as soon as you start off to the target.

We had several early return experts in our squadron and they were universally despised. Sick call and "low on oxygen" were preferred excuses. It was going to be a hell of a long war the way they were going about it.

When I was in cadets, the Army kept screaming that they wanted men who were officers first and pilots second.

I though such statements were a joke. I wanted to be an officer for the extra pay, the prestige and the fact that when you were an officer about 90% of the people in the Army had to leave you alone.

The Army just didn't phrase it right -- what they wanted was character first and flying ability second and I agree with them.

Further, it was my experience that the more combat flying you did, the more tolerance you developed for it.

I once flew seven missions in eight days versus the usual norm of one or two or none a week.

Toward the end of this sequence, I was so physically and mentally exhausted that I was almost in a stupor and impervious to my feelings of disaster.

If someone had told me that a wing had dropped off while we were flying a mission, I would not have particularly cared. Excessive combat flying provided its own anesthetic.

Other books by California Aero Press,
P.O. Box 1365, Carlsbad, CA 92018:

WASHOUT! The Aviation Cadet Story,
ISBN 0-914379-00-3

Aerial Gunners:
The Unknown Aces of World War II,
ISBN 0-914379-01-1